"Be yourself: Everyone else is already taken."
- Anonymous -

(Somewhat different from what Oscar Wilde said)

for JoJo

Copyright © 2016. R. Orlando Marville.

All rights reserved.

This publication may not be reproduced, in whole or in part, by any means including photocopying or any information storage or retrieval system, without the specific and prior written permission of the author.

This book is sold subject to the condition that it shall not, by way of trade or otherwise, be re-sold, hired out, or otherwise circulated without the author's prior consent in any form of binding or cover other than that in which it is published and without a similar condition including this condition being imposed on the subsequent purchaser.

First Edition, September 2016.

Cover Photo by Pelle Hybbinette

Cover Design and Interior Layout by
Caribbean Chapters Publishing Inc.

Set in Adobe Caslon Pro

ISBN (paperback): 978-153-7683-17-1

This book is dedicated to the women who have had an impact on my life, in particular 'Mama', 'Mother', my dear Mother, Mom, Adé, Ollye and most importantly my dear wife, Anita, who continues to be an inspiration.

Table of Contents

Growing Up in Bim 1
Harrison College. 26
Britain and Europe 47
Sweden 76
Ghana. 89
England Again 114
Sierra Leone 118
Cote D'Ivoire. 133
Back in Barbados. 141
Foreign Affairs. 145
Washington DC & New York. 151
Washington DC,
    The Second Round. 167
Caracas 175
Brussels 187
Georgetown. 231
Haiti 249
Barbados Once More 258
Brittons Hill 271
Travels, Mainly in Africa. 295

This book is a memoir.
The events are portrayed to the best of the author's memory.

The conversations in the book all come from the author's recollections, though they are not written to represent word-for-word transcripts. The author has retold them in a way that evokes the feeling and meaning of what was said, and in all instances the essence of the dialogue is accurate.

Growing Up in Bim

I WAS born in a small village named Gilkes' in St. Lucy, Barbados. Gilkes, situated southeast of Bentham's, lies downwind from Mount Gay distilleries. I have more than occasionally told the story where they slap my bottom at birth to make me breathe; I draw in the potent aroma of Mount Gay rum and say to myself: "I think I will live." Then I yell as new born babies do when smacked on the bottom. Outside the small chattel house in the equally small yard, chickens were clucking and in all probability a donkey cart with its iron clad wheels drifted by with a clatter on the rocky dirt road, adding to the sounds of the village, the sounds of village life. The village itself was no more than two acres at best when I was born. My great grandmother's grandfather had founded it. He was a freed slave. He then married a poor white woman whose parents immediately disowned her. When my great grandmother's parents died, her aunt took over the village and sold all but a 2000 square foot plot on which she lived. She would have lost somewhere in the vicinity of 60,000 square feet.

I was born to an 18-year old girl who had finished only primary school, but was bright enough to have been hired to teach at the same school. Pregnancy in that era meant the mother could no longer work as a teacher. This therefore meant that my mother was to have to work as a maid in other people's houses for a long time thereafter. I often thought that my mother was so bright that she could have become a medical doctor or something equally prestigious at the time if she had been given the opportunity.

Barbados in those days, just over one hundred years after the formal abolition of slavery, had not changed that much. Sugar, although less lucrative than in earlier times, was still the largest enterprise in the country. We were still a colony with policies dictated by the colonial government and the sugar barons, a very small segment of the population. A segment of the black population, not much larger than the free Blacks during the latter days of slavery, owned retail businesses or owned small bus companies. However, the majority of Blacks worked on plantations or were maids or farm hands. Life was tough even at harvest time when there was most money to be earned.

Cutting sugar cane manually is an extremely unpleasant job. The sun is mercilessly hot and the blades of the plant are razor sharp. Additionally, any act of carelessness could mean that the sharp tool used for cutting canes, the bill, would slip and cut into the cane cutter's flesh. An old African remedy would come into play. The wound would be stuffed with cobweb and sewn with a needle and thread. If white rum were available, a small quantity poured on the wound would add to the pain. A further quantity found its way into the victim's stomach to mitigate the pain.

There was also the odd blacksmith or shoemaker or bus driver or carpenter or even teacher. While these jobs carried more prestige, they were never such as could make a sufficient financial difference to completely separate these tradesmen from the generality of field workers. Not even the small shopkeepers fared that well. The plum jobs like parish priests or management within companies selling sugar or wholesaling were reserved for the Whites.

My great grandmother delivered me. She was a traditionally (meaning essentially African) trained midwife, who was later to claim that she had never lost a child at delivery. Mama, as the two generations above me also called her, was a gentle old woman. My great-grandfather, Cunjoe Marville, was the flute player in Sam Tuk's band. That somehow makes me a member of a cultural aristocracy, even if a very poor one. He was reportedly the best musician in the band. I seldom saw him, though evidently he took me to weddings at which he played. I have always liked the flute since then. My father was a bus conductor from a Pie Corner family that had had some means, but he was an orphan and that meant that he and his two brothers had nothing, and from early had to go out and work. That was essentially what it was like in Barbados at that time. We lived in a small chattel house with a shed roof. On one side of the house was a paling of galvanised steel. This had been attached to what was initially a flamboyant pole, which grew into a full-blown tree. I suppose we kept that bit of the yard between the house and the back paling enclosed because Mama kept a few chickens. Everybody tried to keep a few chickens or rabbits to ward off total protein scarcity.

I also learnt something about nature in that back yard. Birds often made their nest in the tree. On one occasion when the nest was low enough, I took it down to examine the eggs. The owner of the eggs never returned. It was as if my touch had defiled the eggs and the nest.

Mama was a phenomenal old lady with long hair that seemed to be black and white on the same lock. She used to sing a lot, and was generally so pleasant that when she called you, you could not ever tell whether it was for a snack or for a reprimanding smack. A simple smack said enough. Regrettably, sometimes she called you to administer cod liver oil or castor oil. The cod liver oil when mixed with limejuice was nearly palatable, but the castor oil never reached beyond my lips. I was so good at vomiting at the sight of castor oil that they eventually gave up trying to administer it to me. My two poor cousins were less fortunate and had to stomach that horrible liquid. She cooked and cleaned for us and told us stories at night. Her favourite was an Ananse story. She would sit us all down in semi-circular African style and roll her story out.

Apart from playing hide and seek on moonlit nights or reading by the same moonlight there was little else to do in the way of entertainment. The road that ran through the village was unpaved. Jagged stones stuck out from the well-packed dirt. I must have fallen on these rocks an infinite number of times. To this day, the scars remain. But it was there for us to play on. It was all we had. We were poorer than the proverbial church mouse. It is actually very difficult to explain how poor we were to anyone today, even if the same poverty still exists.

Once in a while during the sugar cane crop season when the sugar mill at Alleynedale was working, we would walk along the cart road to the mill and gorge ourselves with cane juice, which we called raw liquor or with boiled cane juice, which went by the name "crack" liquor. Bim, as I call colonial Barbados, was at that time one very large cane field. We passed on a cart road that always ran between two fields of cane. At that time, one grew a lot of sweet potatoes, yams, eddoes, bananas, cassava and breadfruit. Cane rows were lined with pigeon (Congo) peas, the great protein source that had been brought from Africa along with yams and Guinea corn (sorghum). Guinea corn also grew on every small spot available. The village mill ground that crop along with Indian corn (maize). No wonder Barbados was to be blessed with so many centenarians later on, since these provisions were what we essentially ate. Animal protein came from the small rabbit kept for the purpose or the grizzly-feathered chicken. No one could really afford beef. When one was fortunate enough to acquire a cow, it was for the milk and the eventual calf. If someone else owned the cow and one kept the cow for that owner, sometimes one would receive a calf as compensation. That was village life.

Going to Alleynedale was a fabulous outing for us. We would always return home with full stomachs before going to bed. We would walk back to the village singing for fear that some bogeyman would otherwise rush out from the cane fields and attack us. By that time my two cousins Bertie and Vere had joined me.

Bertie and Vere were the first two children of my Aunt Gwenyth, my mother's younger sister. They were to live with me like brothers from then on until I left to study in London. Bertie was light-skinned like his mother, while Vere was dark-skinned. Vere was a phenomenal talent.

Much later, Vere became a very good cricketer and opened both the bowling and batting for Texaco with the great Malcolm Marshall. He taught the young Marshall some things about fast bowling. He was also an incredible self-taught musician who could sing, play the piano, the organ and the guitar. Having refused to go abroad to study engineering, he learnt enough to become Manager of Roberts Feed Manufacturing Company. There he was the one they turned to if something needed fixing in the old factory, and the one who mastered the computer system at the new one. He picked down the first television my mother bought because he wanted to see how it worked. He then coolly re-assembled it. Vere also had and still has a phenomenal memory. Much later in life, I might call Vere and observe that it was raining. He would then calmly declaim some poem on rain. He could recite the first page of Dickens' *A Tale of two Cities* or of some Zane Grey novel.

Back then, however, there was simply little to do or few places to go in a small, poor St. Lucy village. What we did do—Errol, a fellow young villager and I—would be to wait until it rained really hard and we would climb through the various windows of the bedrooms where we had been sequestered to keep us out of the way and jump to the ground below and run through the village buck naked. I often wondered what had happened to Errol. I figure if he had had the same forward-looking family as I had, he might have done well in life. I met him several years later. He died not long after that.

Anyway, he would get a beating and I a smack with a stern reminder that if I went out in the rain and got pneumonia and died, it would reflect rather badly on Mama. Even in very small poor villages one still had a reputation to look after. Misinterpreting this on one occasion got me a rather stern smack.

For some reason, my grandmother and Errol's mother had fallen out, as one says in a Barbados village. It meant that they did not even say "Good Morning" to each other. I thought that in keeping with my great grandmother's stance, I would also not say good morning. The neighbour promptly gave me a slap. When this was reported to Mama, I got a rather serious smack. I think it landed somewhere about my ear. There was, however, one good thing that came out of it: Mama and the neighbour began speaking to each other again.

Nonetheless, I felt a certain intimacy with my great grandmother, so I did not hesitate to tell her what I knew.

On one occasion I ran to her and said: "Mama, dem set o bitches out dey talking yo' name." Then, she merely laughed.

This intimacy also expressed itself in my sitting on her lap and playing with one of the prominent black moles on her neck. I did this whenever I was sleepy, or simply in need of her affection. Then one day, the mole fell off. One can imagine my absolute horror. It was beyond surprise. I do not think I ever played with mama's moles again.

Barbados' real politik crept into my life twice within my first year. First, the St. Lucy parish priesthood had been given before my birth to a White Barbadian instead of the better-suited father of Errol Barrow, since in those days of institutionalised racism one could not have a Black Bajan in such a position. And so, when my mother took me to be christened and offered the names Trevor Orlando as my first names, the parish priest, who had a grandson named Trevor, flinched and offered the ridiculous Ralphston Orlando Glenfield. It took me until graduation to drop the third name and until later adulthood to change Ralphston to Rashid, the Arabic name meaning "the well guided."

The second incident, if one is allowed to call it an incident, is that where a child anticipates on his first birthday at least some sort of cake, in my case there was a national insurrection. As a result of the repression and economic rape of the local black population, exactly on my first birthday, July 26 1937, an insurrection, euphemistically called 'The 1937 Riots', broke out all over

Barbados. It was held that Clement Payne, a Trinidadian Barbadian was the leading force in the uprising, but it was too widespread for it to have been a simple set of riots caused by Payne's bold speeches.

Colonial government had been totally repressive and the economy of Barbados, based almost entirely on the sugar crop was in serious decline. The population was starving. When the disturbances broke out, people went into sweet potato fields to reap what they had sown, but were otherwise unlikely to reap. Payne had been the dynamo within the insurrection and was later to be honoured as a national hero.

While the first incident was only indicative of what normally happened in those days, the second was to shape the Barbados I was to grow up in. Indeed, coming out of the first situation was one Errrol Barrow who took up the mantle of his uncle Dr. Duncan O'Neale and ultimately became the father of independent Barbados. There were other players, like Grantley Adams, who may have been something of an opportunist playing both sides for his own gain. He ran to Britain immediately after the Payne affair for fear of being arrested for sedition by E. K. Walcott, but later came back after a source of his indicated that Walcott was no longer gunning for him.

He then proceeded to remove Chrissie Brathwaite from the position as head of the League and formed the Barbados Labour Party. He then later sued Clenell Wickham for defamation. Wickham was one of the most articulate fighters for Bajan freedom. He was forced to close his newspaper and spend the rest of his life in Grenadian exile. In Wickham's absence, Adams then adopted a political stance, which seemed to mirror what Wickham had been advocating, but he never really veered from his pro-colonial stance. He will be remembered for defending British colonialism at the League of Nations in 1948, where he was a 'British' speaker. He did however, extend the franchise and became the Head of the short-lived West Indies Federation.

Barbados did not really change in any major way until the late fifties when Errol Barrow broke from the very conservative Barbados Labour Party, and with a handful of rebels like Cammie Tudor and Sleepy Smith, became the leader of the Democratic Labour Party. What changed Barbados forever was his summary introduction of free education. It allowed persons who were otherwise destined to become maids or gardeners to gain enough of an education to be significant players in the society. He did it in typical Barrow fashion. He announced that as of the first day of the new term, no one going to a public school would have to pay a penny. That mandate given, he regularised the decision within Parliament and the Public Service bureaucracy. After that, one white plantation owner asked: "Who is going to pull the pond grass now?" Pond grass was a weed that inhibited the growth of food plants.

Before that, the only opportunity for upward movement was to jump through the window to the sea and find some job in the United Kingdom or the USA, or earlier,

Panama or Cuba. But it was the generalisation of the education opportunity that initiated a paradigm shift in this country. The young Errol Barrow was to follow with other progressive bits of legislation which helped move Barbados from the West Indian country with the highest level of poverty to one with one of the lowest levels of poverty, however one measures this phenomenon.

That right to education became something of an entitlement syndrome, so that later, students talked about what was due to them. They were more concerned about a piece of paper which they call a degree than searching for knowledge that would make both them and their country better and more productive. It was sad that there was no one to take the country to what Barrow saw as the next stage—Singapore.

My early childhood, as it was for a majority of other children in Bim at the time, was poor, but happy. Mama was invariably there with her singing or my great grandfather would take me off to weddings that he played at or just to the local rum shop, where I could get my fill of fish cakes, which somehow seemed better in those days. He would say to the shopkeeper "Give him what he wants" and I would hold up three fingers saying "Three Fish cakes, please." That was about as much as a little stomach could hold and digest.

My great grandfather, the flute player in Sam Tuk's band, gave me some familial connection to Tuk music. His father had arrived in Barbados from Martinique in 1837, probably a free black in view of his name, but still escaping from the discrimination practised even against free blacks in a slave-owning Martinique of that era. He is supposed to have been given a job here as an overseer at a plantation, suggesting that he had some skills. He may, regrettably, have been a slave owner. I loved my great-grandfather and vowed, when once I was old enough, to learn French well. So I did.

My first and only problem was my teachers. In my first year at primary school, my old teacher would say out loud "A B C!" which we would have to repeat and then she would fall asleep. She must have had what we called the 'dropsy', narcolepsy. When she woke up, she would expect us to know the letter D. I got a beating for not knowing. A year later, it got worse. The teacher in the new class was a relative and he naturally expected any family or clan member to learn mathematics quickly. I was merely five and did not learn that quickly. So I suffered from beatings as a result. But outside of the classroom I was happy. I played a lot with my goat Nelly, which was exactly my age; did a few chores and enjoyed whatever morsels of food Mama prepared. Both my mother and father worked all day and I therefore saw little of them during this time.

But Mama was always there, even if always there meant dragging my cousins and me along all over St. Lucy. My cousins in this case were Bertie and Vere. We grew up together in Gilkes and later in Hopeland. We also lived in Brittons Hill, before I went off to University. It meant the usual doses of cod liver oil, which I could stomach with lime juice.

In spite of her matriarchal toughness, Mama was a gentle old woman, as kind as they came. When I was much older, nine or ten years or so, she fell and broke her shin, which refused to heal. She spent sometime in the local hospital, if it could be called that, and came out to spend the rest of her life with her daughter with whom we then lived in Hopeland, just about a mile away. Her rather rapid demise I attributed to her inability to walk all around the countryside. She became sad then. She obviously hated being dependent. Additionally her chattel house had been moved to the peasant lot that my step grandfather had acquired by working at Alleynedale. Her world had fallen apart and she soon died. I now walked a mile and a half to school, first on my own and then with my cousin, Bertie.

Hopeland was a tough time for me and for my cousins. Our maternal grandmother (whom we called 'Mother') was a lot less gentle than our Mama. We had a number of chores, as most children should, but we were poor and the chores centred on that poverty. I had no objection to sweeping the yard, but on Saturdays we had to spend long hours walking to some distant wood looking around for dried tree branches or twigs that had fallen and then late in the afternoon, returning with 'Mother'. If our pickings had been poor, she returned with a single bundle of wood on her head. If we had managed a good haul we all (Mother, Bertie, Vere and I) took bundles on our heads. This was firewood for cooking in a small smoky kitchen. The kitchen was covered with a galvanised roof and the cooking area was a built up plateau with three large stones that somehow sat through many a meal without moving or breaking. We had not yet arrived even to the stage of the kerosene stove. It was therefore dried tree branches or dried cow dung that one used as fuel.

Added to that, Mama had become unable to walk around, so she really wanted to die. She would talk to us, but with none of the fire and warmth that characterised her earlier life. One day she said to me: "Come here son, I want you to do something for me. All I have is this penny."

"Mama," I interrupted, "I cannot take money from you for doing anything for you. You have always done so much for us."

She cried.

When she died, it was the first time I had seen a dead body. She lay there in wake, as many people came by to see her. Then she was buried in St Lucy's churchyard, where her daughter and granddaughter were to be buried several decades later.

In Hopeland, six of us lived in a chattel house with two eight by ten rooms. Mother (our Grandmother) and James, our step grandfather, slept in one half of the house, while my two cousins and I and/our uncle Everett, Mother's youngest child, but a grown man, lived in the other room. It had a deal board table and two rustic chairs and an ottoman. Everett, whom we used to call Uncle Pam, slept on the ottoman when he was there. We had to make do with our share of the floor.

On one occasion I was asleep in the bed in Mother's room during the day and there was a lot of commotion. I felt pain and assumed that I had been beaten. Beds were made of flour bags and stuffed with cuscus grass, a haunt for centipedes. A centipede had stung me and they were trying to get me out of bed to kill the vermin. By the time I was fully awake and cooperating with the hunters, the hunted had long disappeared.

Whenever we helped mother in the kitchen, we realised how smoky the place was. It hurts just to remember what a hard life she had to live. We did not even have an outhouse. At night, one sneaked out to rid oneself of any liquid reluctant to remain within our system and had to use the potty (Fr. pot), if anything more serious occurred. During the day, we would use the cane fields as the public toilet. We also had to go to the standpipe to fetch water to cook with and to bathe.

Mother left me one day to cook the meal for my two cousins and myself. The meal was a disaster, since I managed to pour too much pepper sauce into what was supposed to be the gravy. Naturally, I ate my share, but the two, younger than me, found it difficult to swallow the heavy dose of capsicum I had injected into the sauce.

We also had to go to the Alleynedale yard just before daybreak to fetch the milk, which was poured into the communal pot of chocolate, or chocolate tea as we called it, plus a hard biscuit, which constituted breakfast. My father had provided the money for the milk, which was intended for me; I was quite happy to share it with the others. I remember once waking my cousin who had been sleeping in the late afternoon and telling him it was time to go for the milk. He prepared to go and it turned out to be very difficult to prevent him from almost certain danger since the plantation dogs would have been loose. Then it hit me. Mother, as we all called my grandmother, was not at home and she was always at home that early in the morning. I told him and then he believed me.

All this was on top of having to walk a mile and a half each day to school and the same distance back. If we decided to get in a bit of cricket or football after school, it meant that we had to run the distance home in order to be on time for our chores. As I recall it, my grandmother did not much like cricket. She caught us once playing in the gap, rushed out, grabbed the bat that we had deserted in our flight, and in an attempt to throw the bat at us, threw the thing sideways and nearly knocked out the glass on a neighbour's door.

What made matters worse for me was that there was a young boy called Bounce, who some thought was a spitting image of me. I do not pretend to have been an angel, but Bounce was simply wicked. He threw a stone at someone's dog and I got a beating for it. He took some fish cakes from a vendor at Mile-and-a-Quarter and said his mother would pay. The seller thought it was I who had taken the fish cakes and told my grandmother, who had no money for luxuries like a fish cake. "How dare you go and trust 'goods' in my name?" she asked. Before I could reply I was walloped. I have not seen Bounce since those days, but if I met him now, I believe I would have to pop him one for all the trouble he got me into by looking like me.

Already, Vere was potentially the best cricketer of the three of us, though he was by far the youngest. I was so relieved that the glass-breaking effort had failed. Our backsides would have had to repair the damage she had done. Mother was not an unkind person. It was just that poverty and all the stress she endured from just trying to make ends meet, to raise three boys and to feed her husband and a son who still lived at home made her nearly always angry. I still do not know how elastic the sides of that little house must have been to accommodate all six of us, my grandmother and step grandfather in the small bedroom and the four of us in the equally small only other room.

Our singular pleasure was being allowed to go to the sea (as we call it) with Uncle Pam. His name was Everett, but everybody called him Pam Pussy or some variant of it, so we called him Uncle Pam. He was a good swimmer and so a group of us followed him to Six Men's. There was a pier and the swimmers would walk out to the edge of the pier and jump off. One foolhardy kid followed the grown men out on to the jetty, jumped off and nearly drowned. In spite of this, he repeated the idiotic feat. They rescued him once again. This only gave him the courage to do it a third time. This time, after rescuing him, they beat him and sent him home. The less daring among us were content to play in the pristine waters of the lagoon that was later covered over by a road! The only lagoon I have seen that was similar—though I must confess superior in size—was decades later in Sierra Leone.

In those days in Hopeland, we knew how to make tops out of the fustic tree wood. After shaping the top, we cut the head off a nail and then pounded the nail into the thin side of the top and there it was. We would also cut a young branch of some subtle tree like the tamarind or clammy cherry and stick a mud ball on the end of the twig and swing it. The mud ball would fly an incredible distance. Once when I swung, the ball did not travel. I looked around at my cousin Bertie who was bawling. The mud ball had landed on one of his eyes and naturally shut it. I managed to get it off and the eye opened again, but not before we had drawn the wrath of Mother.

Vere seemed to be the happiest of us. He learnt things very quickly and he knew how to take care of himself. On one occasion when he had infuriated his brother, Bertie tried to kick him. Vere deftly moved out of the way and touched the back of Bertie's heel. It was as if he had thrown Bertie several metres into the air. Bertie fell with an almighty thud on his backside. In a further effort to push Vere into a sweet lime fence, Vere stepped aside and Bertie fell into the fence.

One of the reasons too why we had to get home early, was that if our school uniform had become dirty, it had to be washed and dried and ironed for the next day. Indeed on one occasion, I had put a pen in my shirt pocket and it leaked. It was impossible to get the ink stain out. My mother had to rush and buy a new piece of material and make a new shirt that night. When the neighbour saw the light on at four a.m., she came over to see what was wrong. When she discovered that my mother had been up all night trying to make a shirt without a machine, she too pitched in to have it ready in time for school that morning.

We were all dirt poor in that and other villages. I remember an incident, where a friend with a stub of sugar cane, wanted to share it with me. He told me to hold on to one end of the sugar cane and he would cut it. I thought he would chop down directly on to the stub, but he slid the knife across the slippery surface of the cane and it cut deeply into my left index finger. Blood began to pour and I took a bit of cloth and tied around the cut to staunch the blood flow. My friend panicked. He shouted that I should get to a doctor. It was his fault. His mother would pay for the treatment. Actually, my grandmother fitted the cut skin back together and put on a bit of Elastoplast and it healed. What was strange about the situation was my friend's suggestion that his mother would pay for the doctor. If rubbing two brass pennies together would start a fire, she would not have been able to create a spark. Nobody had any money to go to a doctor. Although my mother worked for two different doctors at different times, I do not remember going to a doctor before I was fifteen. So poor were we all then.

Much earlier, one day, I dug a small hole into my ankle climbing the breadfruit tree outside the gate in Gilkes'. The wound became septic and I had to stay at the General Hospital for several weeks. I evidently enjoyed that sojourn. My mother who came to visit me every day would ask: "How come you have such dirty pyjamas? These were clean yesterday."

I had in fact asked the nurses' permission to feed the little children on the ward. "I was feeding the 'childs'," I replied proudly.

During this time, a German U-boat that had found its way under the net around Carlisle Bay was forced to let off two torpedoes to lighten its load. One hit the Cornwallis, and the other came up onto the beach just a few hundred metres away from the hospital without exploding. The one that struck the Cornwallis opened a hole, which let out lots of tins of corned beef and other goodies that had been absent during the war. Our great local divers promptly retrieved them from the ocean floor and put them on the market.

When I returned to school, I must have become brighter, because nothing we now did gave me any problem. There were few other incidents at primary school other than two involving the headmaster. The first one was when a large group of us, playing war, broke down several sugar canes in the field of battle we had chosen. A paunchy old white man owned the plantation and the headmaster could not treat his complaint lightly. We were warned and I did not return the following day. However, I was accused of being there on both occasions and I was slated for a beating. As the headmaster pounded away at my hand, I let out a scream and peed on his shoes. That stopped the beating. What could be said about that headmaster was that he wrote beautiful poetry in the Bajan dialect.

The same headmaster had a favourite whom he did not think could best me in the exam which one sat to get a scholarship to secondary school, so he persuaded my mother to send me to the Parry School at age ten. That turned out to be a great favour to me. It was the foot in the door moment for me. I completed two forms at the Parry School in my first year, and thanks to coaching by the now Sir Clifford Husbands, I won both a Junior and Senior First Grade scholarship, the latter of which I took up and went to Harrison College.

The path there had been interesting. Mr. Husbands asked if I wanted to have private lessons. I replied that I would have to ask my mother. She, of course, agreed and it was the private lessons that prepared me for the exams.

Before I left primary school, there was one incident, which surprised me in a certain way. The school bully, Victor Bluchie, had hit my cousin Bertie. Bertie, of course, took off and ran home a mile and a half away. To my surprise I decided that I would take on the bully. I knew I could not out-box him, but I believed I would fare much better wrestling him. So I rushed at him. He got in a few blows, but I was able to topple him over and get my legs around his throat. I squeezed until he bit me on the leg, got up and ran away. Victor Bluchie was never the school bully after that. I got home in Hopeland to find Bertie already dressed in his home clothes. He must have arrived half an hour before me.

There were two or three incidents at the Parry School

that I remember particularly well. In my first year at that school, my neighbour copied all the sums I did in a test. He even copied my mistakes, so we were both beaten since he refused to confess. The headmaster, Mr. Smith, was a tough little man and I got to thinking that he liked beating children. It was therefore a bit of a surprise both to Mr. Smith and me that the upper form started laughing out loud one day.

Evidently, Babb, the grounds keeper in the churchyard next door, had managed to cut down the limb of a tree on which he happened to be sitting. He fell with an enormous thud on to the walkway through the churchyard. Mr. Smith might normally have caned the ringleaders in the laugh, but he rushed downstairs to find Babb getting up off the ground. He politely asked: "Babb, you alright?"

Babb was furious. "You see a man nearly break he ass and you ax if he alright?"

The final memory was that one day Mr. Husbands came into class with a riddle. He uttered it very proudly and asked if anyone could solve it. My hand shot up in an instant. "You need to think this one through," he said. That put paid to my hurry and so I assumed that I was wrong. I changed my answer and none of us got it right. I do not believe that he thought that I had not got the right answer, but that he wanted to prolong the process.

The Husbands were, apart from the Barrows and the Brownes, the nearest things to a local black aristocracy. My mother had worked as a maid at the family in Mount Standfast and had, she insisted, helped Clifford with his homework even when he was in sixth form at Harrison College. I had spent some time there with her in the maid's quarters where I would decapitate weevils pretending that I was removing their tonsils, or race bits of paper, which I called boats, down the gutter that ran through the yard.

Evidently, during that period too, my mother was drafted into a cricket match (since she always talked about cricket and indeed bowled to me so that I could learn the game). There were only 21 men, so one of the Husbands said to my mother "You always talking 'bout cricket. Why you don't come and play?" My mother went into the house and changed into a pair of trousers and joined the 21 men.

Frank Worrell, who was on the other team, came out to bat. Nobody wanted to bowl to him so they put my mother on and she clean bowled him in her second delivery. I was never able to better that feat later even though I played cricket for years to come in Barbados, England, and the USA and in three West African countries. And to beat it all, no one else could possibly claim that his mother had clean-bowled the likes of Frank Worrell.

Barbados had become peaceful again largely as a result of the war. We all ate what we grew, which was mainly yams, breadfruit and sweet potatoes, which we called big grain rice. Protein came from peas or beans, which we also grew or from small animals like rabbits or chickens. However, most of the population was still very poor and silently disgruntled. My mother was not one to be quiet. One day after having to attend to me, she arrived late for her work at Alleynedale. The 'mistress', as one called the female white bosses, complained that her lateness had made her have to look after young Timothy. My mother explained in very straight terms that she too had had to look after her own son and walked out.

I am certain that in most cases the offending nanny would have apologised and all would have been well. The social relationship between Mistress and Nanny would have been reinforced and that would have been enough to ensure peace for a long time into the future. That was the era, which I call discrete slavery. I think I owe that stubborn streak to my mother. Nobody bullied her and nobody bullied me either.

There was one other confrontation I had with a bully, when we had moved to Brittons Hill. We used to play cricket on a small patch of land across the road from our house. One day, one of the local boys, Goldbourne, decided that he was not out and that he would lie in the middle of the pitch. I promptly took the hard ball and bowled, as fast as I could. The ball landed in his ribs or stomach. He got up and ran, howling like a little puppy, back to his house. Vere had in the meantime assembled a heap of stones in the event that he had to join battle. I lost track of Goldbourne for several decades. I then ran, after some sixty years, into a nephew of his. He informed me that Goldbourne had taken the window to the sea, gone to England and studied engineering. He now lived in a big house in St. Philip, which meant that the miserable little boy had grown up and now led a successful life.

Harrison College

I HAD won both Junior and Senior First Grade Scholarships and so I was off, on the basis of the Senior Scholarship, to Harrison College. There had been some embarrassment along the way. On the morning of the Junior First Grade exam, my mother had fed me a rich breakfast of eggs and such as I was unaccustomed to. I must also have been nervous at the beginning of the exam. I vomited and had to be provided with a new paper. I passed the exam nonetheless. By the time the Senior Exam came around, I ate little for breakfast and was so well prepared that I came first in the whole island. The late Bobby Morris, who was to become a friend and a colleague on the Harrison College cricket team, was second.

I arrived at the gates of that institution with my mother. The same fate was happening to Albert Braithwaite, whose mother also thought that it was necessary to have a near clean shaven head on one's first day at the college. He also came in tow of a commandeering mother. Naturally, we were christened, as they called it. We had our heads slapped by other boys.

Going to Harrison College meant that I had to move

to the city. There was no way my parents could afford bus fare, little as it then was, to Bridgetown each day. For the first year therefore, I lived at the back of a rum shop in Baxter's Road with two friends of my mother. There I observed some dubious business practices, but I was there to go to school, not regulate business morality. So I walked to school each day and tried to adapt to my new environment.

Soon afterwards, my mother received a job working with a Belmont Road doctor, which meant that from the servants' quarters to the church or to Harrison College was the easiest of walks. The doctor, and consequently my mother and me, moved to Brittons Hill. My mother had a small house there on land rented from the doctor. She later bought the land for what a famed lawyer thought was an extravagant price. But for the first time since moving from Hopeland, we had a place of our very own. My cousins were all to grow up there with my mother and their mother, my aunt.

Brittons Hill was a new experience. I soon had a little girlfriend, Pat, who lived in Henry's Lane. I would borrow my mother's bike to see her. We would meet in the street outside her house and say pretty things. I once kissed her on her lips and went home feeling airborne. I was twelve.

Pat did not swim, but her cousin did. So I invited her cousin to swim in Carlisle Bay, right opposite Henry's Lane. I picked her up to take her out so that we could go for a swim. I stepped on a lionfish or some other fish with a sharp spike down its back and it cut into the sole of my foot with a vengeance. I bled like a pig when I came out of the water. We tied a handkerchief tightly around my foot, stuck the foot back into my shoe and I was able to walk all the way back to Brittons Hill without any further bleeding occurring. When my mother untied the handkerchief, I began to bleed even more profusely than before. She wrapped almost half a roll of Elastoplast around the foot and carted me off to the General Hospital. Arrived there, it was decided that I would need some stitches, so they proceeded without anaesthetics, to stitch up the cut. They said it was not necessary to deaden the sole of the foot. Eventually, they put a nurse to sit on my leg while the stitches were inserted. Young Jeff Kinch put me on a bicycle handle bar and rode off for Brittons Hill. He could not ride up the hill, but was able to push the bike over Brittons Hill and deposit me safely back in my mother's care.

After that, my next girlfriend lived on the far end of the same street where I lived. Like Pat, she was enormously pretty. That relationship lasted nearly up until my penultimate year at Harrison College. Initially, I could not dance and she was a great dancer. While I took lessons, she left me for another Harrisonian who could dance and who had a car. Her brother continued to call me brother-in-law for decades and decried the choice of man she eventually married.

My mother and father had long separated, although they maintained the friendliest of relations. My father had two more sons with two other women before he married the second woman, Hilda, and had four more sons with her and two daughters, though not in that order. There was some dysfunction in that household, since Hilda did not have the discipline of my mother and they perhaps became too many mouths to feed. My second brother was one of the most brilliant kids I had ever encountered, but he never quite managed to make a life for himself. The youngest of the siblings became even more disoriented. The brother, who managed to make a very good life, was Michael who suffered from polio, but recovered and somehow that experience must have driven him forward. He became a refrigeration engineer and has worked for one of the few very successful international businesses in Barbados, the Goddards Flight Kitchen. My number one and three brothers have done reasonably well.

By the time my two older cousins were grown up and left home, my mother had met Douglas Garvey, a seaman chef on one of the regional ships to begin with and then on the Harrison Line. They were married and he would live maybe half of the year at Brittons Hill and the other half out to sea.

Just then my mother became very religious. As a result, I had to go to church three times on Sunday—morning service, Sunday school, evening service—plus two or three nights during the week. Looking back, I wonder how much more studying or even just profitable reading I could have completed in that time. The Church was the Pilgrim Holiness Church at Welches. That finally came to an end when I was about 17. The Sunday school teacher said that personality was just a veneer, nothing substantial or internal. When I corrected him, he simply remarked that these boys who go to Harrison College thought they knew everything! That was it for me. I was in love with the pastor's daughter. Years later I heard that she had had an incestuous child. I was horrified.

When I had reached seventeen, I told my mother that I was no longer accompanying her to church. I was not prepared to accommodate the hypocrisy that pervaded the system. She said that I was a confirmed agnostic (whatever that could mean) and accepted my decision. It was a quality I admired in her. Her husband did not either go to church with her. He preferred to have a drink with friends. She also accepted that.

My mother and natural father retained an excellent relationship even after he too was married, so I grew up with the very unquestioning love of both parents. My father at first lived in a small apartment on Bay Street. (The building is now renovated and houses the restaurant, Lobster Alive). However, on his own, there was no way he could take care of me except during the long vacations, which we still call the summer vacation. His lodgings were a metaphor for Barbados of that period. It had two windows that looked out to sea. Even if one had a job, one tended to look beyond the sea for any real opportunity.

I was old enough to take care of myself during the day, while he worked and occasionally at night, he would take me on the bus where he was a conductor. He also fished from his bedroom window, since the sea came much further up than it now does. He would weight the line and cast it as far as he could.

One night, he went to sleep with the line attached to his big toe. There was an enormous thud, which woke me. There must have been a huge fish on the line. It virtually pulled him out of bed, and the thud was his fall on to the floor. When he got up to haul in the fish, the fishing line broke.

On another occasion, we caught a stingray. I was holding the line and I felt something. At first, my father thought the line had become attached to a rock or something of that nature; then the ray moved and ran around the back of the building. My father sent me down to the beach to haul it in. We managed to do so, but since we did not eat rays, we gave it to someone from St. Lucia.

Dad was a great swimmer. He used, with a couple of his friends, to tie his clothes on his head and swim from the old Harbour Police jetty (somewhat north of the jetty now standing there) all the way to the Hilton Hotel, where they would dry their bodies in the sun. They would then take a bus back to Lower Bay Street. He also taught my two cousins, Bertie and Vere and me to swim. When he thought I could swim, he invited me to go for a swim. The swim took us out to the merchant ships in the bay. They must have been at least half a mile out. Getting there was relatively easy. The return swim was less comfortable. The choppy water filled my ears, beat on my face and had me nearly crying as a result of all the blows the sea inflicted on me. I have always been grateful for the swimming lessons since swimming is a rather comfortable exercise when one has less than functional knees.

My last memory of that apartment on Bay Street was the flood of 1948. The Constitution River was a genuine river at that time. There was a lot of rain, which not only caused the river to overflow its banks and wash away most of the houses on the street that ran between Queens Park and Queens College, now the Ministry of Education. All sorts of stories emerged from that flood. One story claimed that an old lady whose house was washed away had been rescued still sitting on her toilet somewhere in the careenage! The storm that caused the flooding also damaged the building in which we lived. When we woke up in the very early morning to see what had happened, only the stairway from our small apartment to the exit remained. There were no walls standing apart from ours, and those of the heavily reinforced bathroom on the ground floor below us, and right next to the sea. All the other occupants had simply left the building.

My father walked me to Belmont Road, where my mother worked, left me there and said he would be all right. He then walked back into the faint early morning light. He was like that. He would always find his own way. It was like the time his merchant ship sank. He was injured. He found a bit of driftwood, stayed afloat with it until they were rescued.

Throughout this period, I still maintained contact with St. Lucy. My father had two good friends in St. Lucy, a Mr. Phillips, who outlived both my father and the other good friend, Mr. Armstrong. Mr. Armstrong's two eldest sons lived at my father's later when he moved to Eagle Hall, but it was the son of my age, Richard Armstrong, who was my great friend. I would at weekends occasionally borrow my mother's bicycle and ride from Brittons Hill to Cove Bay where they lived. I would ride there on a Friday afternoon and return on Sunday just after midday.

In those days country people believed that there was not much in the way of food in town, so my first evening meal when I arrived would be a rich Bajan soup with one enormous yam accompanied by an equally enormous sweet potato, some salt meat and a dumpling that would have made the Guinness book of records for its size. My mother often said that if she had the choice between feeding and clothing me, she would undoubtedly clothe me, but I assure you I could never finish one of those meals.

At the weekend, Richard and I would occasionally walk over the hills inland from Cove Bay and trek past Pico Tenerife and make our way over to Morgan Lewis. We would eat the wild sea grapes and fat pork that grew on the hillsides and drink water from the springs we found there. When it rained, there would develop a small muddy pond not far from the Armstrong house. We would pretend that we were swimming there. It was in fact too shallow to swim, but the idea of actually swimming was exciting to us. Eventually we became quite good swimmers and could swim in the open sea off Lil Bay. I enjoyed those days. Richard and I became such close friends that even some folk from the Pie Corner area thought we were relatives. We remained friends till the day he died from a ruptured aneurism of the brain.

Harrison College was different from the Parry School in every thinkable way. It was considered more prestigious; it had a lot of white kids who often got into the school because their parents had money. I knew only one poor white kid. He was a brilliant singer until his voice broke. Before that moment, however, he could hit high notes that would have eluded the likes of Mario Lanza. He hung out with the rest of us. He later became a medical doctor. There was one other white kid, Nick Burrowes, who hung out with his black friend. His father, I later learned, was a radical who did not believe in the system practiced in colonial times, although he was a colonial officer. He also acted in plays with the rest of us, playing a page with me in a Shakespeare play. He has remained my good friend to this day. There were a few others who did not much believe in ethnic separation, but informal separation was the rule.

Whites in general, however, kept to themselves.

Then one day, a white twin picked a fight with a black boxer we called Snowball. He beat them until their shirts were all torn, he fighting against two. All the black kids gathered around to ensure that no one from the other side would interfere.

There were a handful of black snobs too. Their father would send a car to pick them up. Most of us would have considered riding in a car a special privilege. There were not that many cars in Barbados at that time. They also ensured that they did not mix with the rest of us. They even considered it acceptable to insult the rest of us wherever convenient.

Harrison College was nonetheless a very positive personal experience. I never got into a fight with anyone; did well in class and began to play sport with some level of competence. I do remember some incidents from my earliest efforts that were at least comical. Like everyone else I began to play football. I do not remember being any good at it. Oddly the two occasions I recall on the football field were not stellar. There used to be something of a feud between a Wiltshire and a Hunte. I have no idea who started the fight on that particular occasion. However, the two pugilists approached each other without realising that I was between them. So after landing about ten punches on my body, they both withdrew quite contentedly. On another occasion, I broke away with only the goalkeeper to beat. I was quite small at the time. I only weighed 99 pounds at age fifteen. Anyway, I kicked the ball with everything I had. The goalkeeper did likewise. The ball went flying back up field and I flew over the goalie's shoulder and landed in front of the goal.

We also managed one historic walk around Barbados, about which I wrote my first article for the local newspaper, the Barbados Advocate. Of course, I was not paid for it.

Two of the fellow students who went on that walk are still with us and are good friends. But three of the more picturesque, Guess Box, Spottie and Spoony have all passed on. Spoony gave me the nickname—it would be a bit risqué to explain why—Toffee or Tofi, as I preferred to write it. (Before that they used to call me the book or bookus and when I missed a question someone might say "Christ, the book misprint!")

Spottie tried on the last day, when we had all made our last change of clothes, to jump over a ditch, missed, landed in the ditch, fell and slid a good distance along it. We called it Sonja Heine on the moss. He had to change back to a set of his dirty clothes. Guess Box just ate a lot and sang calypsos. Spoony was one of the most beautiful people I have ever known. Apart from being an excellent bridge player and later a very successful headmaster at another prestigious school, he was a fine comedian and a totally generous person. We spent some time going into a cave at Welches and disturbing the bat population.

It was with a different group that I now became involved. Richie Haynes and I had made friends with Louis Wiltshire, whose Bajan parents lived in La Brea, appropriately named, in Trinidad. We swam in the water of a nearby beach and ended up with tar on our bodies. One knew how to remove tar. We also went on a fishing expedition off what was then the small village of Chagaunas. However, before we could get a line into the sea, a black cloud signalled the coming of a rainstorm and we hustled back to the shore. We were forced to acquire a few shrimps from a fisherman already onshore to take back to La Brea with us.

The Wiltshire mother, Rose, was one of the most incredible mothers I have ever encountered. They were not poor, but she raised nine children, all of whom achieved something in life. I recently attended her funeral. She was 100 years old, and had spent her last days in Barbados with one of her daughters.

We spent some time there before I moved to the house of one of the Marville uncles in Barataria, Uncle Cosmo. It was the era of *Mama Look a Booboo* and Sparrow's *Jean and Dinah*. My little cousin was prevented from singing *Mama Look a Booboo*!

Later, Louis, Erskine Sandiford and I studied in the living room of Clifton White (since our house was too small and likely noisy) for the Barbados Scholarship.

I am not sure what I liked most about Harrison College. Looking back, I did not think much of the teachers in general, although there were a few brilliant ones like Jeff Lebens, the Burley and three or four competent ones. What was impressive was the intense competition in the classroom, on the stage and on the sporting field. Additionally, there was a tradition that you had to do at least two things, one of which was to perform well academically. The second was normally playing some sport. You were generally laughed at if you could only do one. Guess Box, who was no slouch academically, but who was obsessed with cricket and calypsos, once put his cricket bat on top of the bookshelf. Someone shouted:

"Guess Box, take down your damn' pen!" I believe it was Spoony who came up with that remark. If you did not play any games or act or did something like control the lighting for a play, you were considered a softie.

I played basketball when it was in its infancy in Barbados and eventually played for a Barbados team against a visiting Canadian team. In my final year at school, I also captained the school basketball team that won the national championship, edging out Garry's club. I played basketball twice at night during the Scholarship exams. I did not believe in last minute cramming. In my one match for the national team, the Canadians beat us hollow, even though we had on our team the incredible Garfield St. Aubyn Sobers (Garry), now the Rt. Hon. Sir Garry Sobers and a national hero. He was magnificent at any sport. We used to say that if one invented a sport, within a week Garry would learn it and beat the inventor.

In that game, Garry said "Pass the ball back to me." We therefore drove towards the key and passed the ball back to him at mid-court. After he had successfully hit three shots from the middle of the court, the Canadians put a man permanently on him and shut down our scoring.

I also played cricket for the second Division team and eventually for the First Division, where, believe it or not, the same Garry Sobers prevented us from winning the cup. If we had won the game against his team, Police, we would have been champions. We could have. Our spin bowler, Eddie Perkins could turn the ball an incredible amount and evidently without himself knowing how or when, could turn the ball both ways. He managed to lure Garry down the wicket. Garry missed the ball, but our wicketkeeper, like the great man, misread it too. Garry had only a few runs then. However, he went on to make two hundred runs in that second innings and had us scrambling to save a game that we had been winning right up to his entry at the crease.

We had a torrid time batting in the second innings with Carl Mullins bowling bodyline. He could bowl a bouncing in-swinger that came somewhere between your shoulder and your chin. He got my opening partner, Bertie Smith and Erskine Sandiford both caught in the slips by none other than Garry. I managed to hook at him and survive. It was only, however, when Teddy Griffith, our left-handed captain came in and smashed him for four that things changed. I was now faced with less aggressive bowling, including Garry himself and I was able to hit a few fours and stay with Teddy to the end of the match.

I had grown up in Brittons Hill at the same time as Garry was growing up in the Bay land. We played cricket at Bay Street Boys' as 11-year-olds. He was brilliant even then. We crossed paths fairly often, even when he was in England. On one occasion a Bangladeshi lecturer at the University heard me talking to my Southern Indian friend, Mohamed Muhajiri and I mentioned Garry. He butted in with "Do you know Sir Garry?"

"Yes," I replied.

"Well, if you invited him to a party, he would come?"

"Yes," I again replied.

Then quickly as anything it was arranged to hold the party at Mohamed's house in Rockley New Road. I invited Garry and he turned up alone. He said that he was in the doghouse, so he should return home soon. His wife had wondered why if I invited him to a party, it was not at my house.

Anyway, he never got past the steps leading up to the house. Everybody met him there. Someone asked what he wanted to drink and they kept him busy talking while they fetched him drinks and eats all the while. He never actually managed to enter Mohamed's house. Best of all, the Bangladeshi lecturer said to me: " Do you know what it will be like when I tell my brother that I shook the hands of Sir Garry Sobers?" Garry was the greatest all-round athlete that has ever graced this planet. He played cricket, basketball, football and golf for Barbados. And to my mind, he was the greatest cricketer ever.

I, on the other hand, was not always an athlete to be proud of. I was persuaded to enter a swim meet for my house at Harrison College. I was asked if I could swim 25 metres, 50 metres and 100 metres. I replied honestly that I could. No one bothered to ask how fast. They even asked if I could dive. I replied in the affirmative. For me diving was going deep under water. So they entered me in all four events. After coming last in the first two. I decided that I could swim much faster doing freestyle. So I did, only to hear someone scream "You trying to drown me?" It was my dear friend Austin Ward. So I returned to a gentle breaststroke, which I could have continued for another mile or two. I came in last.

The high dive was even more dramatic. I did two belly flops and disappeared under water for quite a while. I thought diving was going deep under water, not some fancy acrobatics while in the air. After the second one, I believe they feared I might disappear for even longer, if not permanently; so they stopped me from diving.

Harrison College also transformed me from the shy country boy I was to someone a little more confident. I believed it was acting in plays that did the trick. I was taught how to project my voice, and even though I was no great actor, I somehow ended up playing parts in the Green Room Theatre and even once played at the Empire Theatre, where our headmaster, John Hammond, played the lead role. But it was play night at Harrison College that was exciting. I remember that in between acts we would sing out back stage to the guitar playing of Kurleigh King, who was also my first basketball captain.

I got to play Mephistopheles in *Dr. Faustus*, a modern version of the Faust theme, more familiar in Marlowe or Goethe. It gained me all sorts of popularity among Queen's College girls as well as my girlfriend of the time who was a St. Michael's girl. All the play-acting and sport did not detract from my academic work. I managed to gain 8 'O' Levels, to which I added French in my first year in Sixth form. I had been in the Science stream until then and the headmaster had done an experiment whereby science students could do either Latin or French but not both.

Sixth form was special. Mr. Hammond who taught history to us in the school library was more of a dramatist than a historian. Of course in those days we were taught British history and European history with a British bias. I am constantly reminded that the victors often invent their own facts in writing history, a process that occasionally requires decades of research to correct. The Africans put it best in the proverb, which says that until the lion gets to tell his own story, the tale of the hunt will always glorify the hunter. Mr. Hammond was a bit like the hunter. Although he was Irish, he thought that British colonialism was a good thing for the rest of the world except for the Irish. I also did Latin and English.

Mr. Lebens was the English teacher. An Austrian Jew, he was a magnificent teacher of the language and the literature. He even made me believe that I would probably one day study English and would write creatively. However, although I got the highest mark obtained in Shakespeare, I scored a mere 56% in one of the papers, so I chose to study history, where I had got a distinction. I also did well in Latin and in the General paper, so I was awarded a Barbados Scholarship in 1955. There were five such in those days. Some of my contemporaries like Richard, later Sir Richard Haynes, Louis Wiltshire and L.E. Sandiford, now also Sir Lloyd, followed a year later together with the younger Steve Emtage.

Since exam results were published way after the cut-off date for entry to a British University, it was usual to have to wait for a year before leaving for such a University.

In that year, Barbados Scholars were invited to teach at the Modern High School by one of the most progressive educators in Barbados at the time, Mr. Louis Lynch. That year remains special to me for at least two reasons—first, Hurricane Janet and secondly, my stint as a teacher. Janet behaved, as I wrote then to a very close friend of mine, like an unpaid whore. She tore down trees and a building in which several people had gone to shelter just because it was a church. The result was a disastrous loss of life. Elsewhere a man was cut in half by a flying sheet of galvanized steel. In Brittons Hill where I lived, I saw a large roof fly in the near gloom and land on a huge tamarind tree. Night was to fall with the roof still there like some eerie reminder of a tumultuous day.

My teaching stint was at the Modern High School. I was expected to teach a small class in one year what we had taken two years to do at Harrison College. Incredibly, the pass rate was extraordinarily high. I had the pleasure of teaching students like the late Dr. Ester Archer, Nell Britney, Doriel Blackett, and Clyde Griffith. It was a sheer pleasure to see students absorb, with such ease, material which we, in a more privileged set of circumstances, had had more time to learn.

Harrison College was perhaps most important to me for the education that it provided, but also for the fact that most of the friends I now have are people who were at Harrison College with me. I was to run into them again in London, and in the case of one friend, Mickey Walrond, we even ended up living in London together and later travelling about in Western Europe together. I also lived with Nick Burrowes (twice) and with Vernon Smith.

There is one very dear friend from that period, whom I still miss. It is Spoony. His actual name was Keith Roach, but even my children used to call him Uncle Spoony. We were poor kids together at a very early age. We entered a cave in Welches together, disturbing the bats which lived there. We acted in plays at Harrison College together. He was a brilliant comedian. His performances as the Grave Digger or Polonius in Shakespeare were among the best I have ever seen.

He did not win a scholarship and may have been lost in life but for the fact that he decided to do an external degree from London, I believe. I do not know if I could have mustered the energy or discipline required to do this. Spoony succeeded and became the Headmaster of Combermere and produced the first Barbados Scholar that school ever had.

He had a certain graciousness that I can never forget. In 1974, I told him that the removal of Salvador Allende from office had been the work of the CIA. He suggested that some of us always saw a CIA plot in everything. Later, when my statement turned out to be true, he said that he should have realised that I would have known things that I could not disclose. I was in Foreign Affairs at the time.

Later when I was back in Barbados and we played bridge—Spoony was an excellent bridge player—he indicated that his doctor had indicated that he had a heart problem. So Spoony walked miles and miles. When nothing improved, he went to see our mutual friend, Mickey Walrond. Mickey had a look at him and determined that there was nothing wrong with his heart. He sent Spoony to a colleague, who discovered a cancer in his colon, I believe, that was as large as a breadfruit. It was too late then. He was given chemotherapy because he was in such good physical condition.

I was at the CARICOM Secretariat at the time. I called Mickey to find out how Spoony was doing. Mickey told me that Spoony had been buried the day before. He had discontinued his chemotherapy. His partner later said that even in dying Spoony had been the most beautiful person she had ever known. I could only concur. Spoony was indeed one of the most beautiful and unsung persons I have had the honour to know.

As mentioned, while in Brittons Hill, my mother met Douglas Garvey, a distant relative of Marcus Garvey and a chef on a ship, and married him. Dougie, as she called him, always brought her shoes. He was a gentle man, a little too fond of the bottle and an inveterate smoker. In spite of that he lived some 79 years. I wonder how long his liver would have lasted had he drunk in moderation and did not smoke at all.

I travelled with him once around the southern Caribbean and landed in Trinidad. I was travelling with Richie

Haynes and Louis Wiltshire. We spent a memorable vacation at the Wiltshire's. The father, Winthrop, was working in the tar fields at La Brea.

When I left Barbados for London, I continued to see Dougie. Nick Burrowes, my fellow page at school, and now my roommate in London, and I would go down to the docks and eat some delicious Bajan food that he had cooked. Dougie would talk about where he had been. He had been to many places, a few of which I have not yet visited myself. But it did create in me a sort of wanderlust. I remember he once said that if one thought South Africa was bad, one had not yet gone to Mozambique, where Africans were treated like slaves!

Britain and Europe

TRAVELLING TO England was normally done on one of three French vessels which went from somewhere in the French departements to Barbados, on to Puerto Rico and then Spain, before docking in Southampton or somewhere else in Western England. One then took a train to London. I think it was the SS Antilles on which I travelled. Air travel was extremely expensive in those days and my scholarship did not allow for what would have been considered a luxury. So, as one might say, I took the boat. In fact the scholarship funds were paid into the system, so I only received what was left over after board and lodging and what was left over was precious little. Even in 1956 600 pounds a year did not go very far. I worked at the post office at Christmas and picked fruit or worked in a pea factory during the summer.

The journey across the Atlantic was more interesting because of the characters on that boat than the journey itself. Apart from various people being seasick, there was the occasional fun of dancing at a time when the boat listed so heavily that we all ended up on the floor in the orchestra, having to extricate our various body parts from the musical instruments. The musicians, who were evidently more accustomed to these happenings than we, were always quickly out of the way.

There were all sorts of characters. There was a very good Guyanese table tennis player, a Bajan I knew before also en route to London, a Frenchman who changed dinner places each evening and ate enormous quantities of food, and an Englishman who did the same thing, but to deplete whatever wine existed, and a young German girl who wanted me to seduce her. This medley of characters was more than enough entertainment for any transatlantic journey. I somehow could not believe that such a small Frenchman could eat so much. I had seen other people drink as much as the Englishman, but he nonetheless stood out. We stopped briefly at Vigo in Spain, where one of the characters claimed that he had a victory with one of the local women.

Southampton was cold and damp. I learnt immediately that this was a completely different climate. The warm bright days of Barbados were to be a thing of a past that became all the more distant the longer I had to stay in England.

I was enrolled at Queen Mary College, a dainty little place on the Mile End Road in the heart of Cockney East London. My young cousin, Jillian Marville, who is now a podiatrist in New York, was about five at the time. After I had been away for about six months, she asked her mother to write and tell me that I had been away for long enough, so I should come back home immediately. I was not to return to Barbados for some thirteen years.

As I once told a colleague, studying at London and living there meant having a double education: from the University itself and from London. At London, I led with my sports head rather than my intellect. I had chosen History, which apart from my professor was a dull subject, which dealt with British and European history pretty much as if it were world history. Additionally my special area was what was called Tropical Dependencies. Interestingly here, when one dealt with Nigeria, for instance, primary material was British colonial reports, while Nigerian material was considered secondary material. I did not therefore shine as I was expected to.

Quite early in my sojourn in London, the British Council offered Jean Holder and me the opportunity to travel around in Britain and stay with two English families and one Scottish one. Our first stop was in Shropshire, I believe where we stayed with an old lady whose family had been instrumental in hiding Charles the Second. The castle where we stayed made me think of *Lady Chatterley's Lover*, largely because of its size. It was cold inside even though that spring was not particularly cold.

The old lady drove us about the area. One day she ran out of gasoline and Jean hitchhiked to a gas station to bring back a gas canister. In our evident difficulties, a woman living across the street where we were temporarily parked invited us into her home and offered us tea. The old lady declined the tea. I later wondered whether she considered it beneath her dignity to accept tea from someone in the village.

Our second stop was more interesting. We stayed at a young family in the Lake District. The husband was some official in that region and he had a charming wife and two very pleasant children. We all played football on their front lawn and went hiking by the lake. Jean maintained contact with the entire family. Much later, I gather the husband had died. His wife visited me on my first year in Brussels, stayed at the Residence and swam in the pool. I was pleased to return the favour of entertaining someone who had been such a gracious hostess.

Our third and final visit was to Scotland. We hiked a lot there too. However, what I remember of that visit was that in a single day, there was rain, sleet and snow and the sun came out in the evening.

Back at Queen Mary College, I immediately became something of a star. Funnily, I was announced as two fast bowlers from the West Indies, R. Orlando and G. Marville, thanks to a Bajan priest twenty years earlier. They had to be satisfied with one R.O.G. Marville, who was a medium pace cum spin bowler, who thrived in the English conditions, where anyone could swing a ball all over the pitch. I also batted at number three. I had enormous fun playing cricket. My History Professor, Bindoff, an expert in Tudor History got wind of my cricket prowess (for what it was worth) and asked me to play for the staff team, which was desperately in need of a swing bowler. We had lovely lunches and teas and I got to hobnob with my lecturers, including Dr. Leslie whose little daughter was quite a character. On one occasion when she was obviously bored with the soft drinks she was allowed, she said mockingly, "Would anyone like another glass of dry lemonade?" What was even funnier was when she saw her father's eyes follow ever so briefly a rather attractive young woman walking by. She said to a rather embarrassed father, "Not a bad bit of crumpet, eh Dad?"

One memory of college cricket I recall was playing against an Oxford team—I believe it was Christ Church. The wicket was a dead flat wicket and I decided to liven it up with a bouncer. The ball struck the batsman in his jaw and had pretty much the effect of a knock out punch. He wobbled and gratefully did not fall. When I approached him, he waved me away, again wobbly, saying: "I'm okay, I'm okay." I then bowled a straight, fast, ball on the off stump and he was clean bowled.

Then of course, I played table tennis and field hockey for my college. I was not good enough at either to play for the University. I could have played cricket for the University, but too much of the sport was played when it was necessary to study for exams. I also played basketball for the University of London and eventually won the University Purple for my performance.

Basketball was played in the winter, as was hockey, so that did not cut into exam study time. I loved basketball and wondered what would have become of me had I opted for Harvard or Yale or Stanford. That was an idle thought, since in those days, it would have been considered non-U to go to an American University, so stupidly colonised we were. I did however enjoy playing for London. Regionally, we were the second best team, since we could never beat the YMCA, which had a former Hungarian centre who was a great player. But we always beat Oxford and Cambridge with our very highly multinational team. Apart from the US contingent and one Brit, we had a Swedish Tunisian, a Hungarian, a Canadian and myself. We even played and beat a Nottingham-based US air force team who fed us well after the game. They also took us back to the train station afterwards in one of their coaches.

But London outside the University was a bit of a shock. The most immediate thing that struck me was the absence of hygiene from any action. Women would spit on a handkerchief and wipe their babies' faces. When I left the hostel and went to share an apartment with Mickey Walrond and a Guyanese medical student, the landlady told us that baths were free. She thought that we would bathe once a week. When she discovered that we bathed every morning, she put a meter on the hot water! We fiddled with the meter—yes the statute of limitations has run out on our misdemeanour so I can now confess—and had a bath every morning, as we would have done in Barbados.

London then was extremely dirty and this was compounded when there was thick fog or haze, called smog. It was on such nights impossible to use buses, as they had to be guided by policemen on foot! I once even tried to unlock the wrong door along the street. When I lit a match and put it against the number on the house, I lived three houses further up the street.

John Hammond had always given the impression that Brits were so sophisticated that I expected a lot more than what I encountered even among the students with whom I lived during my first year at college. (He had told me that I should go to London since I would not understand what they said at Oxford or Cambridge!). The institution had put me together with Nick Burrowes, who although he had at least one English parent, insisted he was West Indian. He had grown up in Guyana and Barbados. He was a great roommate both then and later when we lived with Vernon Smith in Hackney. The British students at the hostel all assumed that it was an error to have put the two of us together, so they would ask Nick about me and he would come back in good West Indian style and relay the titbits to me.

There was one incident outside the hostel which highlighted the attitude towards us. Three Swedish girls studying English at London invited Nick, Steve Emtage and me to a party. The girls were returning to their university in Lund, Sweden. They had also invited an English student.

The party was quite pleasant until the English student decided that Nick was his kind. When Nick rebuffed him, he said it was because of colonials like him that England had a bad name in the colonies. We all thought this very funny.

He then proceeded to tell jokes, which fell so flat that no one even smiled. In a last ditch attempt, he decided to read a passage from Shakespeare's Richard the Third. Steve thereupon rose to his feet, spread his arms and declaimed the entire passage from rote. The English student left at that point in utter defeat.

On the street, it was not much different. Coming from a Barbados that was still largely segregated, with trespassing a crime to be brought against any black person found in Belleville or Strathclyde after dark, one would have imagined that London would have been easy on the psyche. Yet it seemed that people went out of their way to be racist. At a bus stop a man asked me where I came from. When I replied Barbados, he informed me that there were some coloured people (what a euphemism!) who lived in his building. You could tell that they were coloured by the smell of their cooking. I explained that he was probably talking about Indians or Pakistanis. He asked how he was supposed to know the difference between one coloured person and another. I suddenly realised that the British saying that all Chinese look alike also applied to all black people.

On another occasion when I was with my British basketball colleague, we were speaking to a man on the street. When I spoke, the man indicated that he did not understand what I was saying. John, my Cockney colleague, was flabbergasted and put in: "But he speaks better English than either of us." It became immediately clear to me that he did not think he would understand me and therefore he did not.

London had been flooded with Caribbean immigrants

after British losses in the Second Great War, so there was a desperate need for other low-paid workers to fill the gap. The poor had been the bulk of the cannon fodder during the war, and now the poor from a starved British West Indies were brought in as bus conductors, nurses, street cleaners or whatever. They immediately caused a stir among the British working class, the upper class being all too far removed even from their own working class to bother. The former group thus disliked the West Indians. An unscrupulous pack of landlords also preyed upon them, putting them in run-down areas of London along with the worst off among the British poor.

And then there was Oswald Moseley, a neo-fascist, who further fanned the fires of racism. The outburst was to come some two years after I had arrived in London. A mixture of teddy boys and working class thugs, who attacked a 'mixed' couple, started it. The violence spread and five young Brits savagely beat up some West Indians and were given four years in jail. While it may be thought that this was to send a message to all other racists, it was nothing of the sort. The police were clearly also in on the act.

Richie Haynes found himself at Notting Hill Station wanting to continue into the township. He asked a couple of policemen to escort him a little way down the street. They simply responded that the only place they were willing to escort him was back to the station. This apparent anecdotal incident was reiterated in one form or another throughout the process of the Notting Hill

Riots, as they became called. When later the Notting Hill Carnival was instituted to display West Indian culture in an inclusive friendly way, it was the police once again who caused things to go astray, unable as they were to distinguish between revelry and rowdiness.

I was fortunate not to have been involved in any of this. I do want, however, to highlight the bravery of our Jamaican brethren, who stood up to the attackers and made the aggressors retreat.

From then on, Jamaicans came to be regarded as those to be feared. All West Indians when asked if they were Jamaicans tended to reply in the affirmative.

After living with Nick for a year in the student hostel, I lived with Mickey and another medical student in Hampstead. Mickey was a phenomenal companion. I have seldom come across anyone with a more varied set of skills. He claimed that he developed his interest in literature and politics from me, but I developed an interest in photography as a result of his photographic skills. When he was dissatisfied with his prints, he would simply cut them up systematically to make lampshades. He also did geometric painting. What though was particularly impressive about him occurred as a result of the Government of Barbados refusing to extend his scholarship for one year so that he could do a separate degree in anatomy. He therefore saved a bit of money going into his additional year and then proceeded to play bridge and poker and earned himself enough money for the entire year. He augmented this with waiting tables.

His savings therefore remained intact.

London, however, was much more than racist attacks on black people. It was the British Museum with its wealth of discreetly acquired and stolen artefacts and *objets d'art* from the world over; there were the great Halls of Music, where I heard Marion Anderson and Paul Robeson, released from his internal exile in the USA; it was a place of learning not easily parallelled in any one city elsewhere. It was the halls of science at University College or Medicine at Guy's Hospital or Economics at LSE. It was Hyde Park and Speaker's Corner; it was Oxford Street with its glittering shops; and it was the home of Whitehall, which controlled our destiny through its colonial office.

It was more of this London that I got to experience when I went to live in Hampstead and walked on the Heath and frequented the pub where George Lamming and Christopher Fry were the two local celebrities. Indeed, when I was falling asleep one night instead of studying, I decided to run in a wood to the north of where I lived. The window to my room leaked and I could no longer bear the smell of burnt paraffin I had to use to heat the place. A policeman stopped me and asked what was the matter. I explained and he said that he had a colleague also studying for exams and he too was in a fit. And so off I went. Another night I ran into the same officer and he simply asked how the exam was going. Such an encounter would have been unlikely in Notting Hill or even Hackney, where Nick, Vernon and I later lived in what was called a flat. In fact, one night as I was on my way home in Hackney, two officers stopped me and asked where I was going. I replied that I was going home. They proceeded to ask my name. I replied that unless they were charging me with something, they could not ask me my name. Realising that I could not be intimidated, the two men wished me goodnight.

There was one other Shoreditch incident, which was rather revealing. Vernon and I went one night to a pub, where the publican refused to serve us. We left, and at Vernon's suggestion, filed a complaint to the Board responsible for licensing pubs. When the day came for examination of the case, the publican appeared with an attorney. Vernon, who later became an attorney, suggested that I should speak to the issue. I did. The publican in turn lied: he claimed that the reason why we were not served was that we kept banging our coins on the table. I pointed out that I was proffering a ten-shilling note! He later produced an old black woman whom he claimed was a personal friend.

In the long run the adjudicator decided that there was no clear case of racism. I indicated that I did not mention the issue of race. I then proceeded to walk over to the publican, saying: "Let me be the first to congratulate you on the renewal of your license." He held out a trembling hand. Sometime later, we returned to the pub, this time with Mickey. Mickey was of the view that it was such an uninteresting establishment that we should never have found ourselves there in the first place. They served what we ordered this time around.

It occurred to me that it was not only the element of race that played its part here. There was an innate class-consciousness that mattered. One day while I was teaching at a school in Shoreditch, I realised that I had only enough bus fare to get home and that the bank would not be open when I needed to go to school in the morning. So, at lunchtime I took my four pence and a bus and went to the bank. I took out about five pounds, forgetting about change for the bus. The conductor was understandably annoyed that I gave him a pound for a 4-penny ride back to school. So he began a rant. I informed him that as someone doing a public service, he ought to know how to behave. "What did you say?" he screamed.

"It doesn't matter." I responded.

"Well, for you, it doesn't, but in this country, it does," he continued looking for support from the occupants of the bus. Typically, no one spoke up for him. So he fished out as many coins as he could and handed them to me. I thanked him without any fuss. He became even more furious, since he had evidently anticipated that I would complain.

The next time I got on his bus, I only had a ten-shilling note. He mumbled, but said nothing and gave me back my change. The third time, he held on to my chair and rocked it. I ignored him. The fourth time, he brushed my shoulder and said: "There was a bit of dust on your shoulder, Sir." It occurred to me that he figured from my demeanour that I was someone he needed to call 'Sir'.

It struck me then that classism had had multiple origins in England. Apart from the traditional notions of class engendered by feudalism and its continuation into the industrial era or the classism that grew out of slavery in the Caribbean, with classism and racism merging to the point where racism was sometimes practised by black on black, in England this was compounded by the Norman conquest of England which introduced classism even into the structure of the language. I remember an English textbook which we used at Harrison College. It pointed out that while the animal was in the field, it was called by the Anglo-Saxon name ox (ochs) or cow (ko, kuhe), while on the Lord's Table it became the Norman French beef (boeuf). A similar class transfer occurred with the sheep (schaf), which became mutton, or the French word when on the Lord's table. Was this perhaps the same phenomenon that motivated the conductor to call me sir? Did he think that I was, as one said, 'posh' or a toff?

But it was fun living in Hackney with Nick and Vernon. We took turns at cooking. Each one of us fancied being some great cook. We also had two interesting neighbours. He was Trinidadian and his wife Cockney. We all got along fabulously. There was only one odd thing about the wife. If an important visitor came by, she tried, as they said, to put on a posh accent. The funny thing was that it always came out Irish!

There were two or three other incidents that I should perhaps record. I was going out with a German *au pair* young woman who lived with a Jewish family. The family was furious when they discovered that I was black. Her mother was coming to Britain to see her and they suggested that the mother could stay with them. This changed when they asked what the mother would think of her boyfriend. She replied that her mother would probably like him. They withdrew the offer to accommodate her. What was totally absurd about this whole affair was that my girlfriend once told me that her family had known an SS man during the war. Although her parents had been decidedly anti-Nazi, they refused, after the war, to give up the SS man to the authorities. They could not do this to an old friend.

The second incident was equally strange, though earlier. I had met this girl at a summer camp and we became involved. When her mother got to know that I was from the Caribbean, she disapproved of the relationship. However, when my girlfriend was knitting me a sweater for my birthday and was unlikely to finish it on time, her mother pitched in and I received the most beautiful baby blue sweater I have ever had. Her mother did not think it proper for her to be late for my birthday, even though she disapproved of me. Someone later stole the sweater in Stockholm.

I recall that outside this area of dark prejudice, there was some genuine fun in the activities, which I shared with sporting college mates. We used to have what was called a cricket week. It was about ten days long and somewhere deep into Essex. We all slept in a barn with beds arranged in two rows. We played tennis in the morning and cricket later in the day. At night we frequented the one pub in the area. There were two young women there and about 15 of us.

Whoever went out with one of them would come back and find some level of disarray in his sleeping arrangements. Someone would tie a knot in his pyjamas or, in one case, throw his mattress onto a beam in the roof. To get it down, he would have to throw a cricket bat at it and hit it several times before it would fall back to earth. Interestingly, I too had a fling with one of the girls, but came home early enough to avoid any discomfort.

It was even crazier in winter when we travelled to play hockey and rugby. On one occasion two of the hockey players chose to bring along their partners. One of these was actually the player's wife. In true fashion, the rugby players began to sing rugby songs, which were at least R rated. The player with the wife was most embarrassed. The one with the girlfriend was highly amused. I must confess that I was a bit embarrassed for the two women, who had to bear it all the way back to London.

I also met Harry. Harry was a happy young man from deep in Lancashire. He studied chemistry and played the guitar. We teamed up singing calypsos and ballads at school affairs. We decided that we would apply for a fund that was available to students for educational travel during the long summer vacation. The interviewing panel asked what brought a science student and a history student together. I replied rapidly: "Our common interest in humanity." The response did not seem to make much sense to me later, but it got us the award so we could travel to Asia possibly, hitchhiking.

We were thinking of going all the way to Israel, but ended up in Turkey, where Nick Burrowes, studying to be an engineer, was doing a "stage" at a large Turkish factory in Ankara. Our progress had not been as rapid as we had envisaged, so we felt that Turkey was a suitable turn around point.

Harry was a riot. He was about 5 inches shorter than me, and blonde. We were a genuine odd couple. He also took everything thinkable including a cooking pot. On top of his enormous rucksack, he had strapped on his guitar. He had an incredible sense of direction. Brussels is not an easy city to get around, but we walked to the World's Fair in Brussels, 1958, and he made his way directly back to the small hotel where we were staying. Someone stole my travellers' cheques at the fair, so we left Belgium a little poorer. My mother, however, soon had some money wired to me.

Harry was not too gifted with other languages and he immediately embarrassed everyone at a Belgian table. The host had been gracious enough to suggest that we stay at his house for the night. In an effort to thank the family for a fine dinner, he said something with a meaning embarrassingly different from what he thought he was saying. What he said translated to something like "I am banged up (pregnant)."

We continued on, and arriving on the border with Italy found that our language skills no longer worked. We needed somewhere to sleep one night and seemed to have been somewhere in a village. I tried to speak German to two men dressed in military uniform, but they were Italian and spoke no German. I decided to concoct some form of pig Italian, so I said "Voglio lito de una vacca." They rolled on the ground in laughter. I did not know then that the Italian word for barn was much like the French word grange. I suppose that what I said must have translated to something like "I want the bed of a whore." I had used the word vaca (cow), meaning that I wanted a barn. So we went on and knocked on a door. A middle-aged lady came out and Harry gave a sign of wanting to sleep. She asked "Fumi?" Harry immediately understood that that meant: "Do you smoke?" and shook his head vigorously, even though he did smoke. We were shown to a room, which was piled high with hay. We climbed onto the haystack, lay out blankets and prepared to sleep. Soon, a man and a woman came in on a Vespa. Harry whispered: "Don't even breathe. We do not want to have to explain to them how we got here".

We went east from there and ended up in Venice. We took a gondola up the canal to the Piazza San Marco, which was so beautiful that I cried. All that I had read about Venice and its independent Doges, who traded with the Turks and had made this floating city-state so powerful, had in no way prepared me for its beauty. Interestingly, when I visited it again some thirty plus years later with my mother and my son, the canals had become so dirty and polluted that there was no life in them; the city was sinking and Venice seemed only to be a shadow of its former self.

Harry slept little at night and therefore often fell asleep during the day. Our first bit of really good luck came in Switzerland when a man who had given us a ride took half of Harry's stuff and mailed it back to England. The second bit was rather different. Harry insisted that he would not fall asleep but would sit up front for a change. Our driver was German-speaking. Harry began by commenting on a good stretch of road with "Die strasse ist gut, nicht?" Our host/driver agreed: "Ja."

On a bumpy bit of road Harry intoned: "Die strasse ist nicht gut." He had managed to go from "The road is good, no?" to "The road is not good." He then fell asleep, bumped his head on the steering wheel and the driver claimed he was turning off, so he put us down and continued straight on.

Oddly, this was fortunate for us, since our next ride came with a German who spoke, beside German, English, French and Serbo-Croatian. Joachim Muller had been in the Belgian Congo during the war and had fought on the side of the French. He took us all the way to Belgrade. Our first stop was at Bled, then a beautiful little city. Jock took us to the nightclub and then to the small casino. An Englishman came up to us and asked if we were English, I replied in the negative, but Harry agreed he was. The man then fed him so much slivovitz (plum brandy) that Harry became tipsy. He went to the band that was playing and told them that Harry Belafonte was there. They did not believe him, but I was invited to sing. I did a few of Belafonte's songs, which were known everywhere. When I returned to my seat, a Yugoslav said to me "I do not speak much English, but Drink!" He filled my glass with slivovitz whenever I looked away. Jock was drinking heavily too. So at the end of the evening the three of us walked with heavy feet back to the hotel. I remember that the effort of getting into bed was like doing a high jump. Perhaps the only positive of that night was that we met two beautiful students from Belgrade. The one we were later to meet on our way back was Smelijana.

When we arrived in Belgrade, Harry was about to photograph a military establishment of some sort when a policeman came up and told him he could not. Instead of merely saying "Oh" and moving on, Harry tried to explain that he had in fact not taken any photograph. The policeman understood no English, so he took Harry in. Fortunately, Jock, our host/driver was easily found. He explained what had happened and Harry was free once again.

Belgrade was fun. We swam halfway across the Danube and then back. After our return, Jock treated us to a memorable dinner. Harry and I both thought that the ample serving of tasty fish was the meal, only to discover that there was a huge chunk of meat that followed. However, in his very early twenties, such an underestimation is nothing for a male stomach.

From Belgrade we got a ride all the way to Istanbul, Turkey. We bumped into two Germans who were taking two Mercedes cars to Turkey and we gladly went along with them. Passing through Thessaloniki in northern Greece, we were stopped by a crowd of people in the heart of the city who insisted that we play. Traffic came to a halt and a policeman came up to us and said that we were doing nothing illegal, but our performance was blocking traffic. We moved into a cul-de-sac and played for a while. Our Germans wanted to proceed so we had no choice. One man in the crowd made us promise to stop on our way back at some club, which we did and we performed. Greek hospitality was incredible throughout our crossing of the North of that country, whether we were hitchhiking in a car or truck or simply a horse-drawn cart in anticipation of something quicker.

We arrived in Istanbul, an incredibly beautiful city, with its famous blue mosque and lots of minarets peeping up at the sky from varying points in the city. There were also remains of other civilisations in the aqueducts and other relics within the city. We had difficulty ordering anything to eat, because we did not understand one word of Turkish. The waiter took us into the kitchen. We pointed at various foods and we were accordingly served. We took the train to Ankara and went directly to Nick's factory. Practically throughout the journey, a Turkish soldier dressed in thick khakis fell asleep and put his head on Harry's shoulder. Harry was more than relieved when we pulled into the station in Ankara. He had been afraid to move and wake the man.

At the gate we had another of Harry's displays. He said softly to the security guard at the gate that we wanted to see the manager. When the guard raised his head in Turkish fashion indicating that he did not understand, Harry said the same thing louder as if the man simply had not heard. He also tried writing his request. Someone who spoke English finally bailed us out. The Manager indicated that as long as we had a friend (Nick) working there, we could stay as long as we wished.

Not long after we arrived, I went off on a walk and inevitably got lost. Harry was not there to help me, so I chose the best dressed man on the street to ask the way back. He raised his head in the usual fashion, so I tried in French. Again he lifted his head so I tried in German: "Sprechen sie Deutsch?" I asked. This time he did not lift his head; he simply asked in return "Sprechen sie Turkish?" I could only laugh. He was essentially right. Here I was asking him if he spoke English, French or German; unable really to speak any of them, he asked in German if I could speak Turkish! I finally found someone who spoke English and it was remarkably easy to get back to the factory.

Harry got himself arrested for the second and last time. He, Nick, a Cypriot friend of Harry's and I went to a park one evening. We started to do a dance with one person performing in the middle of the ring. A police officer waited until Harry got into the ring and arrested him. This time it was the Turkish Cypriot who saved him. He argued that dancing was allowed in any park anywhere in the world and he was simply giving Turkey a black eye. Unwilling to commit such an infelicity, the policeman released Harry and we stopped dancing.

The way back to England was less eventful largely because we had to part in Yugoslavia. We were hitchhiking on a truck between Ankara and Istanbul when the German owner of the truck stopped it and insisted we come with him in his Mercedes since he opined that it was only Allah who prevented Turkish drivers from having more accidents. We returned to Greece where we performed in Thessaloniki as we had promised. It was at a nightclub and they fed us and put us up for the night. I even sang a Greek song that I had learnt on the way there. The next major stop was Belgrade. Harry had eaten some unwashed grapes from a field even though I had warned against it. So he had a serious stomach problem.

We established contact with the student, Smilijana, whom we had met in Bled. Her father was a doctor and he sent Harry to a hospital on a boat on the Danube. When the nurse asked Harry to take off his pants, he was more than a little hesitant. But he did. On the second day, as soon as he arrived, he began taking off his pants to be scolded by the nurse. "Not so fast, young man." It would take a few days, but Harry was in good hands, so I left Harry in Belgrade, as I wanted to visit my girlfriend, Liv Gladheim, a Norwegian track athlete, in Oslo. I remember once when we were in England, we were somewhat late for the bus we wanted to take, so I suggested we run for it. She matched me stride for stride right up to the bus. She was worth going to Norway for. So I hitchhiked all the way to Oslo. Distance eventually killed that relationship.

We had spent all of the summer vacation abroad. When I arrived at College, there was Harry, wearing pointed Yugoslav shoes, a British blazer and tight-fitting German trousers. He came running across the square to embrace me, as if we had not seen each other for a decade. Regrettably, after we left QMC, he joined the British navy and we lost touch. I liked Harry. He was funny when he wanted to be and sometimes even funnier when he did not intend to be funny.

We both finished our respective degrees, me in History and he in Chemistry, with no idea how this would benefit humanity, but aware that we would have to go out into the world of work. I realised that if I did not teach or leave Britain, I would have to go into the army and do what was called national service. I had tried out the army one summer and that had been more than enough. One lived somewhere out in the middle of nowhere with a bunch of young men with nothing more to do than peel potatoes and follow orders that did not make sense. One was expected, when ordered, to paint coal white. I was prepared to get out of bed and step on a bit of board that floated on the pool of water that had gathered in the tent during the night, or even peel a pile of spuds, but simply as a matter of blindly obeying orders, I was not prepared to paint coal white. It somehow offended any sense of reality that I had at the time. So I knew I was not going to join the army.

So I found a place to live together with Nick Burrowes and Vernon Smith in Hackney. Nick was in his final year and Vernon also taught in the school system. It was easy to find a job as a substitute teacher in one of the new horrors called comprehensive schools in the East End. The British Government had lumped together a series of poor secondary schools and called them comprehensive. It is true that one could do 'A' levels at such schools, but I found myself teaching one student for French A levels in a school with over one thousand students. Most students wanted to get out of school and find a job selling fruit or the like in what they called a barrow.

Normally, substitute teaching meant that one was moved from one school to another fairly often, but I was able to stay at that school for a full year. It had mainly to do with the fact that I started a basketball team at the school and had about twenty students prepared to come to the gym and learn the basics of basketball two or three evenings a week. I was not paid for it, and the headmaster, who was not particularly fond of West Indians, appreciated what this did for the school, so he kept me at the school. Eventually, we were able to put together a team that played against other local schools. We did not normally win, but the kids enjoyed the competition. Evidently, however, when I left for Sweden, the captain of the team got into a fight on the court and kicked someone on the opposing team in the head, and basketball was banned at the school.

There were three other Africs at the school including one South African, Mac Maharaj. Mac was keenly anti-apartheid. He was much later to become an ANC member, spend quite a few years on Robben Island with Nelson Mandela. He was also when not in prison, the leader of Umkhonto we Sizwe, the military wing of the ANC. We joined him in a boycott of South African oranges. A number of English teachers were quite happy to desist from eating the oranges including the one very religious man whom I loved. He thought apartheid morally offensive so he was happy to oblige. The red-faced gym teacher would not join us. He said that he thought that apartheid was wrong, but he could not do without his oranges.

I was to meet Mac twice after teaching with him at Shoreditch Comprehensive. The first time was at the United Nations. I was in the Barbados Mission to the UN and he had come to the UN on things South African. I was pleased to see him and asked where he had been all those years. He had replied quite bluntly: "Robben Island." We chatted a bit. He informed me that he would be returning indirectly to South Africa. The next time I met him, he was a Minister in Nelson Mandela's Government. I was with a trade mission to South Africa. We have spoken since then and communicated by e-mail, but never met in the flesh again.

Mac was not the only South African I met in London. I also met Miriam Makeba at a party. I also met her once again not that long before she died. She was singing at a concert with Hugh Masakela in Brussels then. Hugh I had met even before. He was all in love with my cousin Pat Bannister and she with him. Hugh remained a friend from that time onward. He had interestingly called my cousin to propose to her (after years of being afraid of being rejected by her father) on the day before she was married to someone else.

Hugh stayed with me on one occasion in Maryland and we met a few times in New York. On one such occasion I introduced the Mighty Gabby to him. There was a warm exchange with Hugh asking Gabby after one of that calypsonian/folk singer's long notes, whether he had an extra pair of lungs in his legs! While in Maryland too he met my children who thereafter called him Uncle Hugh. They were most delighted to see him practice on one occasion in a studio in New York.

The third last time I met him was probably in Brussels. I caught his eye on stage and signalled that I would like to see him. He signalled back that he would be back stage after the concert where he and Miriam Makeba were performing. We did meet twice briefly before. I only met him a few times later in Barbados. He was there one Crop Over, found Gabby and asked for me. I was in Guyana and returned the following day, where we got together. I met him once again in Barbados, where he asked about my cousin Pat. I informed him that she had died years before. He then asked after her sister Yolande, whom I telephoned and she spontaneously invited us up to her house for a meal.

Returning to Shoreditch, Mac Maharaj, a Jamaican, an

African American and a Trinidadian actor completed the group. We enjoyed each other's company. Also occasionally in the group were two female teachers who were English, but felt more comfortable with us than with the generality of their compatriots. Interestingly too, the kids at the school invariably flocked around us. That we cared seemed to matter enormously to kids from a deprived area.

There was one hitch. It took four months before I could be processed and paid! After two months, I was broke, but I was able to take a part-time job working at the post office, where I was paid weekly. This involved working both days, at the school, and nights at the post office, sorting mail. So I had about two hours sleep per day. After about a week, I could take it no longer, so I told my colleagues at the post office that I would take a nap on the empty bags and that they should wake me when the supervisor came around. Evidently they saw him coming too late to wake me, so they shovelled some bags over me and told the supervisor that I had some stomach problem and had to be running to the "loo" from time to time. He bought that and left. They woke me and briefed me. That few hours of sleep served me well. I remained in pretty good form until the end of the Christmas season. The pay helped me to survive until the end of January when they finally paid me for my teaching. I thought I would be rich, but with the tax and having to repay my friends, I was still scratching dirt. But I had learnt one thing. You get on with whatever you have to. You simply cannot beat back gravity with a stick.

Sweden

WHILE I was in England, I met two Swedish students, Torsten and Elisabeth. They both invited me to Sweden for the rest of the summer. My dear mother provided the wherewithal and I flew for the first time, to Stockholm. I stayed for most of the time with Torsten's family in Solna. It was a pleasant peaceful stay. I also visited Elisabeth's family in Uppsala, a pretty university town where I met the later to be famous Kerstin Johansson, but she spoke no English then and Swedish was very much a foreign language to me. We wanted to communicate, but could not. I loved Uppsala with its English Garden and its student ambience. It was a clean town of the sort that I had not encountered in Britain.

When I had finished at Queen Mary College, London, I took the additional year of scholarship available to me in Stockholm to do a course in political science. Stockholm was a new experience. From the unhealthy cold rooms of London, Stockholm with its clean street and evenly warm housing was almost like changing continents. At the time, Swedes seemed to assume that if you were black, you were either a musician or an athlete. That was less irritating than the dumb comments that one had to suffer in London.

One last memory of London had little to do with London other than that is where we began the journey. I had tried to get a young Trinidadian steel pan player to join us on an improvised European tour. He wanted to visit his sister in Spain. Sadly his plane flew into the solid rock of the Pyrenees while we were on the road to Stockholm. We drove all the way to Stockholm where we anticipated that it would have been easy to get a gig. We had Edsil Reid on guitar along with David Trotman, I sang and Vernon Smith played the base steel pan. Nothing much happened in Sweden other than that we ended up sleeping in a tent outside Stockholm. However, on our way back, while in Copenhagen, we encountered someone who wanted us to play in his club. What was phenomenal was that Vernon Smith was fast asleep even when we began playing. He never played that drum better!

Contented, we moved back into Germany where we visited the Reeperbahn. The Reeperbahn was a sort of red light district as well as an entertainment hub. We were on the side of the road when a German gentleman came up to us and asked if we would play at a party he was giving. We accepted and were taken to his place by two vehicles. Once there, we not only played but also were treated as honoured guests. We must have played until three or four a.m., when we were put on a bus headed back to the centre of Hamburg. We continued to play on the bus and a few old ladies on the bus evidently enjoyed the music as they tapped and bobbed their heads.

Arrived back on the Reeperbahn, we started to play and a couple of policemen decided to stop us. When we suggested that we could play something special for them and so did, they told us we could have the key to the city.

That was a memorable trip, which could have been even more memorable if we had not lost Stephen, a bright young Sino-Trinidadian football playing student and pan man, in a plane crash.

Returning to my sojourn in Sweden, I learnt fluent Swedish in about six months. My method was new to me, but since it worked, I thought I should describe it. It was basically immersion, but in an ordered way. I first learnt a handful of basic words like to eat or to talk, plus all the irregular verbs like to go, to be and to have. Then I went to a park and tried to speak to children aged between six and eight. They normally use about 200 words; they speak the current dialect and they will correct you if you say something incorrectly. Then you return to adults and it is remarkable how much of the language you can then control.

Even before that, I had gone to the International Club, run by an Englishman who spoke perfect Swedish. Non-Swedes were allowed to become members of the club, but all Swedes had to speak one other language. The young woman I eventually partnered with spoke Swedish and German. I did not speak any German at the time, so I was forced to learn Swedish to communicate with her. When we were alone, sign language helped enormously, but in a park, for instance, it was slightly embarrassing to use sign language. My extra lessons with the children helped immeasurably.

Additionally, I always said to my fellow students that I spoke French. I had really learnt French from speaking and listening to an Italian friend in London. I improvised from my school French. He had lived in Paris, and although he was in London, he spoke little English and I spoke at that time even less Italian. The handful of Swedish students that studied French, spoke French to me; the others, deprived of the opportunity to practice their invariably good English, spoke Swedish to me. Within six months, I could carry on a conversation and listen to the radio, both in Swedish, at the same time.

There were three incidents, which, although I was not unduly bothered by the cold, made it clear that this was not my ideal climate. Sweden has three large glacial lakes. The smallest of the three, Lake Mälaren houses a large archipelago, on which Stockholm is partly based. One beautiful summer day, a girlfriend persuaded me to go for a swim in the Mälaren. When there, she jumped off a rock and swam out a bit. I asked how it was and she replied: "Wonderful!" I jumped in, and if I could have jumped directly back up out of that icy water, I would have. Instead I had to swim quickly around the rock and climb back onto shore.

The second incident seemed at the time to be more

serious. In my first winter in Stockholm a large chunk of my hair at the side and back of my head on the right side fell out. The students at Domus, the rather luxurious student hostel where I lived, called me 'Flintskalle' or Baldie. I ignored them and went to the doctor. He opined that it might have been the fact that I normally had more vitamin D from the sun and that was missing in a Swedish winter. He promptly injected vitamin D into my scalp. I also had the opportunity of asking my friend Mickey Walrond who had now finished his MBBS, but all he could tell me was to name the condition as alopecia areata. Winter passed. In spring, baby hair, softer and longer, started growing out again. I spent a lot of time cutting it back. By summer, I had my full Afro back once more. But then, the following winter the left side dropped out. I did absolutely nothing and it grew back in spring.

The third incident was a little more comical. It was a bright winter day so I went out without a hat or any such protection for my head. When about two miles away from Domus, snow began to fall heavily. I could not get any taxi because every one that passed had an occupied sign on it. People in their homes had a real advantage on me. So I walked back to Domus. When I reached home, my head was covered by a large ice cap. Fortunately, the Afro was able to keep it away from my scalp. It took some thirty minutes of running hot water to wash it all out! I never went out again in winter without a hat.

I stayed on in Stockholm after I had finished the course. I taught English within the school system as well as adult classes and in one special case a single old person who perhaps really enjoyed hearing English and needing to practise it rather than learn it. She was special. She had been the friend of the wife of one of the Nazi hierarchy. She had visited Germany during the pre-war period and had met Hitler. She gave him short shrift. According to her, German aristocracy intimidated Hitler. At one highbrow dinner he could merely say "Ja" or "Nein", never really daring to say anything substantial. However, in the stadium with the ordinary crowd, he bellowed and ranted, feeding off the energy of the cheering mob.

I also sang in a nightclub. I was in that process privileged to meet two Caribbean musicians famous in Sweden at the time—Touchie Grant, a Guyanese guitarist and Rupert Clemendore, the best drummer I have ever heard. Rupert had done records on the xylophone and guitar in Trinidad before. Touchie sang in small clubs. Rupert, who was a perfectionist, scared most Swedish musicians since he would walk out of a session if any professional musician made a single mistake. He often played for visiting American musicians. Art Blakey once allowed him to play drums and Rupert did his famous mix of Caribbean, African and jazz rhythms so well that Art Blake never let him touch his drums again.

I also modelled for Electrolux. They evidently thought that my physique matched that of a fisherman and I could hold an outboard motor on one shoulder and a small shark in the other hand. Funnily, I turned up to a class in a secondary school and there was a poster of me attached to the door. The students wanted so much to hear something about it, but I ignored it and it never came up during the lesson where we talked about boxing, a very topical subject in Sweden at the time. There was one racist incident, but typical of Sweden, it was possible to deal with it at several levels.

I was refused a work permit. My bank, which received monies for me from abroad, also said that I received no monies. I contacted the press and they paid me for writing my story. Later I was invited to participate in a TV programme featuring foreigners and Swedish authorities. The public officers did not know what we were going to ask, so when I asked a question about deportation, the immigration official went all over the place without answering. He later asked me in the dressing room what I was asking. I indicated that he knew quite well. Thereafter, instead of going to one office to leave the request for an extension and receiving it from another, I went to one office and I received a duly stamped passport at the same point.

The whole affair had sprung from an incident where the daughter of a wealthy Swede had claimed that she was pregnant for a Mozambiquan student and teacher. He was fleeing the Fascist control of his country by the Portuguese colonists. He said that not only was he innocent, he was prepared to do a blood test to prove it. No one listened to him. They instead proposed to deport him and in the process sweep up a few black foreigners to deport along with him. The press took up his case as well and he was allowed to stay.

One of the joys of continental Europe at the time was the possibility of hitchhiking any and everywhere. On one specific occasion, I did not even have to hitchhike. I ran into two US students, one of whom had bought a car in Paris. His friend, a Greek American wanted to travel to Athens. They asked me to come along with the two of them and I did. I think they felt that my languages would be helpful. We hardly needed anything but English until we arrived in Rome. Bill, who was driving, said: "Watch me out-Italian the Italians." So he managed to change lanes from the far right of five lanes to the left. And there at the end of it was a policeman. The policeman looked at the number plate and assumed we were French. He was frustrated. So he banged on the hood of the car and exclaimed: "I stupidi franchesi!" Bill asked what he had said and I informed him that he had cursed the French, thinking we were French. Capo, the Greek American was highly amused, but did not laugh until the policeman had disappeared.

In Athens, it was blazing hot. One often thinks of the tropics as hot, but I had never experienced that heat before. Capo took us to the Acropolis etc. and we had a great time in spite of the heat. We even ran into a pleasantly drunk actor who played dark roles, as well as Anthony Perkins, who tried to hide from us behind a glass door!

We returned to France, where I stopped off at the Cote d'Azur and later hitched my way back to Sweden. I enjoyed Sweden. It was the country where I first had to take care of myself. I lived in a dormitory hotel, where each student had his/her own room. There were no restrictions on who came to see you, when or whatever. The hotel/dormitory had rooms with very comfortable beds, a table and chairs and a fully equipped bathroom. The room was always heated at about 18 degrees Celsius. There was a restaurant on the ground floor, a hall upstairs where dances were held. In the basement, there was a photographic darkroom and an old-style Western saloon, replete with a swing door.

The saloon was like something straight from the movies. There was music and sometimes, the odd fight. The fight was often between Svante, from Northern Sweden and Göran from Skåne in the far south of Sweden. I can think of no other country where the southern and northern dialects of the language are more divorced from each other than Skånska and Norrländska. So these two rather large gentlemen often fought when they were saying the same thing. On one occasion I had to point this out. I do not know if they bought my argument or if they were simply too drunk and too tired to continue, but they stopped what was about to develop into a fist-fight. On another occasion, Vince Williams, the powerful but gentle African American who was bartending that night had to stand between them and beg them both to go home.

Characters from the saloon cropped up again and again in my sojourn in Stockholm. Göran played poker with a group of us. He was famous for having once said that he liked dogs better than humans, but then he preferred horses to dogs. He was appropriately studying to become a vet. His poker playing was lousy and he ended up owing me about 10,000 kronor as a result of wanting to play double or quits after owing me a more modest sum. He never paid his debt. One memorable night of poker occurred in the music room of Domus. The only problem after we had procured the room for the entire night was what music would be acceptable to everyone. There was a jazz fanatic and a European classical music fanatic. They both wanted their kind of music. We finally chose the Modern Jazz Quartet's *No Sun in Venice* and played that LP all night. I broke from the game, as I almost invariably did. They were not very good players.

One other denizen of the saloon who stood out was a Yugoslav medical student named Conrad Basner. Conrad was quite a pleasant chap even though his Swedish colleagues did not much like him. He often in that period drank a little too much. He gravitated to me since we were both foreigners. Interestingly, when decades later I returned to Stockholm for an operation on my knee, I called him and he turned up to take me out of the hospital after the operation. He invited me to his apartment where he cooked a sumptuous meal and we chatted for hours, bringing the old times back to life.

On one memorable night in that saloon, José, an exiled Spanish pianist, was playing on the salon piano. Karen, a rather objectionable Swede, decided that his beautiful playing was a distraction. She asked him to stop playing. José turned to me and said: "Orlando, go get your drum."

I was happy to oblige. He played Latin music and we continued until about 3 am. Just about everybody else stayed, but Karen left in defeat.

I also sang and danced a bit. I did a show with one of the great South African dancers, Graham Tatum. I also drummed with someone who has become a great friend, a Sierra Leonean, Ahmadu Jah, who went on to become a famous drummer/musician in Sweden and fathered Nana Cherry and a lot of other musically talented children. We never played at the Domus saloon, but we played in the Student Union's Cosmos very often. There I had one fan, Tatiana, a Yugoslav student who called me her brother. She once won about 10,000 kronor, a lot in those days, and asked if I needed any money. I replied in the negative, but she then suggested that I should keep the money and give her some when she needed it. I obliged and she remained throughout my sojourn in Sweden my fan and my sister.

There was one other money earning activity available and that was being an extra in films made in Stockholm. The first of these was a Swedish film, Svenska Floyd, a parody on the Swedish boxer, Ingemar Johansson. Lill Babs, a pop star, was the lead in the film. She was a very pleasant person. In a second film, I played the Nigerian Ambassador in a William Holden film, The Counterfeit Spy. The final small part was centred on my wedding. It was an Italian film about young people in Europe, called Mullamondo. I saw that film in Barbados.

In the process of exploratory living, I was also taught

photography by an American professional in return for his occasional use of the dark room at Domus. I did not disappoint him. I went on to win the first three prizes in the black and white student competition with two portraits and a shot of birds flying away from a small park on Vallhallavägen.

Sweden was very special to me. It was the most impressive European country that I had experienced. People believed in being clean. There was a progressive bent to the country. Even one of my conservative political science professors, Professor Gunnar Hecksher, who was considerably less ideological than most rightists of the West, would have fallen into that category. I felt free in that country. I even did crazy things that other students did, like swimming in Lake Mälaren, the glacial lake that encompasses Stockholm and joining other students at their parents' summer home on 'midsommarafton', the theoretical beginning of summer, which normally turned out to be so cold that instead of dancing near the ubiquitous small lake, we sat inside, close to an electric heater, and played cards.

I also thought of marriage. My first choice was an Ethiopian beauty, but a Swedish actor snapped her up. There were no other African or Caribbean women around, although there were several African and African American males. So I gravitated to a beautiful young Swede who was working class and might understand my own views better. She had qualified for University but decided to do a Secretarial course so that she could get into the work force nearly immediately. We got married and moved to London where she did a course in modelling, but almost as soon as she had finished, I was offered a teaching job in Accra, Ghana, where it was unlikely that she would be employable as a model. So she went to University there. I also later enrolled to do a Master's in African Studies.

Ghana

GHANA WAS a very important landmark in my development. It was an epiphany for me. Whatever I had learnt including photography came into play. Additionally, and perhaps of greater importance, my political sensitivities were awakened. It was incredible to be in a black country, which had been independent for some six years before I arrived there, while the first leader of my own country did not want to cut the British yoke.

Ghana is not a small country. We had been led to believe that it was very tribal. However, the first person I asked where he came from, meaning what part of the country, answered very proudly: "I am a Ghanaian." Ghana was in several ways very familiar. It was not a land of great mountains. Only one small town East of the Volta River could have been designated a mountain town. Evidently, the indigenous groups fleeing the advances of nations like the Akan, had fled there later to be absorbed, but still retaining their original language along with adopting the language of the conquerors.

The country stretched from coastal towns like Takoradi, Cape Coast, and Accra and Keta, northward through forest, which included the second city of Kumasi. East of Accra was the country of the people of the Gbe language, including the Ewe. One crossed the Volta River at this point and there was the only mountain of the area, where the Gbe had nestled, Amedzofé. It was like encountering a higher Mt. Hillaby in Barbados. The view back to the Volta after it had passed through the dam was breathtaking.

Something ought to be said briefly about the dam. It was one of Nkrumah's signature achievements. It had been finished one year ahead of schedule and well under cost, a phenomenon most unfamiliar in any country especially newly independent countries. To the East, the coastal road stretched to the border with Togo.

The boundary with Togo was one of the very artificial frontiers created by European colonisation. After the First Great War, the territory held by the Germans and called Togoland was redistributed between France (Togo) and Britain (The Gold Coast, Ghana at independence). The division split villages in a way that left some families striding the frontier.

North of both Ewe country and Accra was the forest. From Accra northward one encountered the pleasant escarpment area of Aburi, which the British colonials enjoyed. Indeed the word malaria, meaning bad air, came from the belief that that illness was contracted as a result of breathing the foul air of low-lying land.

Then the vegetation thinned and the landscape morphed into savannah for a long while before becoming Sahel or semi-desert with the largest northern city being Tamale with Wa, the capital of the North-West and probably the area from which our own national hero Busia (Bussa according to British lexicography) came.

While we come as Africans of the Diaspora from present-day countries between Mauretania and Angola, culturally most of our remaining traits in Barbados, Jamaica (partly peopled by Bajan enslaved in the 1600's), and Guyana and to a lesser degree Suriname come from the Akan of Ghana. Even the physical landscape of South Eastern Ghana seemed like somewhere in Barbados. Physically too, people seemed familiar. The very first person I saw who looked like George Lamming, who I think has a near unique face, came from Ghana.

I was once too greeted by an old lady in Elmina, the site of the largest slave fort, built and run by the Portuguese until the Dutch took over and a lot of mixed Ghanaians appeared, some with Dutch names. The old lady greeted me in Akan. I returned the greeting. Now, greetings in Akan or in other African languages are not simply "Good morning, how are you?" but are more extensive affairs before they get to "How is the family?" I followed all the way until she got to the family, where I replied in Akan, "I am from the West Indies." I realised she had mistaken me for one of the young men from a distinguished Elmina family. She then looked at me as if to say, "We send these children overseas and they come back pretending to be from somewhere else." I could not be sure that that was what she was thinking, but I thought it served the look-alike right. How dare he go around looking like me and deceiving old ladies? Fortunately, unlike Bounce of my childhood, he did not get me into any trouble.

There was one other factor in Ghana that was most fascinating. It was the women. It was not that they did not have affairs or bed down with men. It was their actual power in the society. They controlled the entire local food market. They owned the farms, the trucks, the drivers and even a few selected students at the University of Ghana where I was enrolled. Such students, referred to as being on Makola (the main market in Accra) scholarships, were not only the paramours of a particular market woman, but also future employees on a rather large market.

I remember one Saturday morning going to Makola to look for some fruit. The only thing plentiful and cheap enough for my pocket was an orange; I stopped and asked the cost of the oranges. I noticed that one of my students was standing there. He whispered to his mother that I was a teacher. I still only asked to buy some oranges. She proceeded to supply me with oranges, grapefruit and pineapples, the latter two of which were in short supply and thus more expensive. If I was her son's teacher, this generosity was in place. So highly respected was education. It was more like the Barbados I knew when I was at primary school.

The women of Ghana were indeed phenomenal. The Akan, who constitute about 40% of the Ghanaian population, are matrilineal. Inheritance passes from a man through his sister's children. Indeed one of the most brilliant of the Ashanti military leaders during the fight against the British was a woman, Yaa Asantewa, the Asantehene. It is said that when both Kwame Nkrumah and flight lieutenant Rawlings were Presidents of Ghana and had to make tough economic decisions, they consulted the market women, in advance of their actions. This may be an apocryphal tale, but it says something about the power of those market women.

If a young graduate, returning to Ghana with a Master's in his special subject—as was normal—went back to his village to find a spouse, he might choose someone with a primary education. She would be able to read and write and be pretty much like someone who had had a primary education in Barbados 50 years ago or someone who had left school after completing a secondary school education today. He would take his new wife to the University or adjoining area. He would probably tell his wife that to begin with, he probably needed 35% of his earnings for clothes, entertainment and the like. The young wife would take the remaining 65% and put away 10% of that sum a month, while looking for some area of business activity that she felt would be well remunerated. This could range from retail, the creation of a new business or whatever was legitimate. Within a period of 6 to 10 years, she would be earning as much or more than her husband. In the period, she would have borne two or three children and he would have been promoted. If he were a whiz kid, he may have reached a professorship in that period. He now tells her that he needs to use a little more of his earnings to grace his new status. She could easily tell him that he could use all his salary for personal purposes as long as he remembered birthday gifts etc. Interestingly the marriage may have survived an affair on his part, but he has been generally respectful. The day he forgets and says something terrible about her parents, for instance, she would pick up her two or three children and return to her village. His standard of living would take a deep dive.

I was fortunate that during the spell in London, my wife and I had met a young Ghanaian lawyer, who along with his Swiss wife, was also on his way to Ghana. They helped us adjust easily. Nat was from a wealthy Accra (Ga) family and one of his relatives was a Minister of Government, who was so careful that he hardly ever talked to Nat about anything. The fact that they were related was however comforting.

Ghanaian President Kwame Nkrumah had managed to transform that enormous country, approximately the size of Britain or New York State, into the driver of progress in Africa at the time. Beginning with a mere 19 institutions of higher learning, with only one college, he had managed within a few years to increase that number to 108, including three Universities. To do this he had recruited teachers from all over the world. He hired Russians as well as US citizens, Canadians and Brits, most provided as Peace Corps volunteers to Ghana. Nkrumah had the US and Russian contingent teach Science, but never allowed them to teach any of the Social Studies programmes. I taught history, mainly African history, which I was simultaneously learning, and English at an old rundown school named West Africa Secondary. Nkrumah had also decided that other Africans, including those of the diaspora should be paid as Ghanaians. The one difference was that we were provided housing of a very decent standard. Our own housing improved from a house in a compound near the Nkrumah Circle with one other house and three Peace Corps teachers to an upstairs apartment in a newer house with the same teachers.

Later, when I changed schools to another in the city, we moved to yet another even more modern apartment off the Ring Road, this time with Russian teachers occupying other apartments in this modern apartment block.

If Ghana was my political epiphany, teaching at Accra Secondary School was the beginning of the process. Nkrumah was left of centre, but decidedly not a Communist. He was essentially an African nationalist, who had brought back to Ghana with him, George Padmore, a West Indian, and later an Afro-American as his advisors. But the old guard in Ghana did not much like him. Although the Headmaster and senior teachers at the school did not dare say it, they hated him. They were much more attuned to colonial Ghana.

The students, on the other hand admired him. A single incident exemplified the situation perfectly. The Government had put out a request for blood to replenish the national blood bank. The school management downplayed the request for schools to be involved, but I mentioned it in class. One student got up almost before I had finished and said: "Sir, we are from the Third World;

we know what we have to do."

Teaching there was rewarding. Those students who were not the brightest were eager to learn. One student stood out. He was probably the best student I ever had the privilege to teach. I gather that he had explained the notion of an idiom when the French teacher was unable to explain why the French said something in a completely different way from English. However, in my class it was when I asked the students to stop writing about snow and other things they had read about in books and write about their own village or about someone they knew, that that student, Samuel Donkor, a wiry little fellow whom all other students respected, wrote a story about an old man in the village. The description was eerily real. I asked him if he had written anything else. He said he had written a few stories. I managed to get some of them published and paid for. He told me that he would write later in life, but that he would study something more immediately productive, like Engineering. Of course he obtained the best grades the school ever had.

There was one hilarious incident. I was teaching the students to play cricket on the small school ground. We had managed to scrape together two cricket bats and a genuine cricket ball. One of the students hooked a short ball and it sped across the road outside the school. A taxi driver blew his horn at the ball, but neither he nor the ball managed to stop, so the ball became stuck in the car's grill. He got out, noticed the ball and drove off with it, ending the practice.

But most of my experiences in Ghana were of a more serious nature. It was difficult not to become involved in the dreams of Nkrumah who spoke of an African Union of independent states, with a single currency and common market, free movement of its peoples etc. Now several decades after his death, only the African Union has evolved, but free movement of people exists in ECOWAS, the Union of West African States and three Southern African States have a common national anthem.

At the University too, there was talk of Egypt having been the origin of the civilisation that we shared, but most, including an African-American lecturer nonetheless believed that the Egyptians were white. Simultaneously one of my fellow students in the African Studies Master's programme was establishing information to show that West Africans had come to the Caribbean more than a thousand years before Christopher Columbus. It was an intellectual scene of great contrasts. But it was unlike anywhere I have subsequently lived. It was a vibrant intellectual milieu.

It was simultaneously a place with a thousand eyes watching you. When Nkrumah began, he travelled anywhere in the country, but then his opponents began throwing bombs. None of them actually hit him, but they did kill some people. Nkrumah did not have the guilty executed; he put them in prison. But he became wary of going anywhere and his 'people' started being officious and spying on anyone. A friend who was a physics lecturer at the University was picked up one night while we were in a bar downtown. Evidently, we had been talking when the national anthem came on the television. Mark was arrested by two such spies and taken to Military Headquarters. We followed him. He was almost immediately released. The Military and the Police eventually overthrew Nkrumah when he was abroad.

One young intellectual who returned to Ghana at that time was Ayi Kwei Armah. He became a close friend. Years later when he had completed his first brilliant novel *The Beautyful* (sic) *Ones Are Not Yet Born* he wrote articles for a local newspaper. The Military Government considered his writings critical of them and he had to flee Ghana for his survival.

He went to the British High Commission to get a visa to the UK where his sister worked for an Embassy. His interview went rather strangely. Asked what he did, Ayi Kwei responded, "I am a writer."

"What is that?" the British Officer asked.

"Like Graham Green," Ayi Kwei continued.

"I think you just want to go to London to find a job," came the insulting reply.

"I was not aware that there were jobs set aside for people who look like me."

The officer walked out. Jeune Afrique, the then famous African magazine published in Paris, heard of his plight and arranged to have him come to Paris and write for that journal.

He once took me to visit his grandmother and in his normally creative style introduced me as the child of one of those they had taken away in slavery. The old lady said to him with pointed finger: "You make sure that they do not touch him ever again!"

It was difficult after that not to feel welcome. So I jumped into the idea of playing basketball for the University and cricket for both the University and the country. I did a photo of Ayi Kwei for the back flap of his novel *The Beautyful Ones Are Not Yet Born* after I had done more extensive photography for another young Ghanaian writer who was still at the University. This was Ama Ata Aidoo. She asked me to do a cover for her first play *The Dilemma of a Ghost*. I had not seen or read the play, but she assured me that if I came to a performance at the University I would be able to do the cover for her book and a back flap cover of her. I went to the production and took several photos including one which later photographers built on. The hero was pondering his situation. I printed that photograph and after much fiddling in the dark room, lent me by my dear friend Salifu Dakubu of the Physics Department, I was able to reverse it to give the impression of a man stuck between two opposing versions of himself. The publishers actually paid me for the effort, though they later did not pay me for the back flap photos of Ayi Kwei or of the Kamau Brathwaite collection of poems.

In Ghana too, I got to meet some very important people of the time. Dr. Eric Williams came on a state visit and at a reception held at Osu Castle. I met both great personalities, Dr. Nkrumah and Dr. Williams. Osu Castle was a slave castle owned by the Danes. It was one of two castles situated right on the beach outside Accra. On one occasion in the eighteenth century, a rather slick man from the interior of the country came to the castle to buy guns, brought along with him a supply of gunpowder and whatever one then used as bullets. He managed to overpower the guards and take over the castle. The Danish governor escaped and ran naked several hundred yards down the beach to the British castle. The Ghanaian held the castle for a year.

At the castle Dr. Williams shook my hand and said nothing. Nkrumah in his deep melodious voice welcomed me and seemed a bit disappointed when he asked if I were Ghanaian and I replied that I was from Barbados. The castle affair was otherwise merely the usual cocktail party.

More interestingly, Henri Hervé, a French journalist who had been living in Paris with the daughter of the great African American novelist, Richard Wright, was invited to Ghana. He promptly married her and migrated to Ghana. He was the editor of the French version of *The Star*, *l'Étincelle*. I occasionally did photographs for that newspaper. His guest for one afternoon was Malcolm X. I sat on the floor with my camera in front of me. I wanted to photograph Malcolm. Maya Angelou came in late and accidentally kicked my camera. No harm was done, but instead of apologizing, she asked if I was one of those so-called Negroes. She had the caged bird within her, but it did not yet sing. I have loved her work, with which I became familiar many years later.

Malcolm X had just returned from Mecca and China

and explained his evolved philosophy. He no longer spoke of blue-eyed devils; he said he had prayed in Mecca with blue-eyed brothers. His visit to China had also indicated that the oppressed in China were like the oppressed Blacks and others in the USA, all ultimately oppressed by the same monster. He also said that he did not expect to live till age forty. He was shot to death soon after in very mysterious circumstances. A US TV station was set to show footage of the scene, but was evidently persuaded to shelve the programme. But for that day and one night later, very attentive ears heard Malcolm X.

His next appearance was at the University. He spoke in what was one of the largest university halls I recall seeing. It was so packed that several students had to stand outside on the balcony surrounding the hall. Malcolm began his speech with "Brothers and Sisters, Friends..." and continued his invocation in a deep raspy voice "...and Enemies." The students in the hall were from that point on, a captive audience.

Legon (the University campus) was a hive of activity. I normally hung out with Ama Ata and Ayikwei, the two most famous of Ghanaian writers of the time or alternatively with my friend, Salifu Dakubu and his crowd. One night when a group of us had to go to the airport, we ran into someone we knew and asked him what he was doing at the airport. He was waiting for Che Guevara. So we waited too and met the great revolutionary. Che was a little man with a charisma that belied his size. He spoke at the University in Spanish with Roberto Blanco, whom I later met in Havana, interpreting. Ayi Kwei's girlfriend, a Puerto Rican medical doctor, said that the interpretation was not great. I could not tell. It was simply an awesome event.

My private life had taken a different turn. My wife, who had been sexually abused as a child, had never divulged anything about it. She fell into a trap that such victims often become entangled in. We were not doing very well financially, even though she was the best manager of scarce family funds I have ever encountered. So, a well-known African American persuaded her that he would buy our old car. He invited her to his hotel and raped her. Of course the rapist left Accra and she fell into a traumatic state for several weeks. Nothing was ever the same again since she blamed me for the rape. However, we did manage to sell the old Fiat and buy a very old Volkswagen.

Things went on from there but at a considerably restrained level. She was a great student and she managed to reach the final exam. I knew she had done well, but she was unsure and asked me whether if she failed or got a poor grade I would still love her. I replied with a resounding yes. A few days later, she was informed that she had merely missed getting a double first in French and English. She ended up with a first in French and an upper second in English. I was sure it was only because they marked harder in ex-colonial countries so that no one could question their quality. She promptly packed up and went to the YWCA for a few days before leaving for

Senegal to teach at IFAN. Not all that long afterwards I received information from Sweden that we had been divorced.

This made me determined to finish my MA, which had suffered during this period. I gave up teaching and lived in the house of Salifu Dakubu. He was like a brother. He normally lived at his girlfriend's apartment in the heart of the University. I also lived from one job as a host of a fashion show, or from odd photography jobs like weddings. As they say, I hit the books. I was the third best in the programme. Above me were a superb female Ghanaian athlete and an African American who has remained a friend to this day. He was able on his GI scholarship to do a Ph.D. in London. I wanted to do the same, but I had to teach to survive and therefore the only time I could visit the British Museum, where the information I needed resided, was when I had to teach.

Just before my wife's departure, there had been a military coup d'état. While Nkrumah had been away at a Non-Aligned Conference in Indonesia, a group of Military officers staged a coup claiming all sorts of infelicities on the part of Nkrumah. He was supposed to have robbed the state of millions. Yet all they could find in his bank accounts was something in the nature of 148,000 pounds sterling. Interestingly, Nkrumah had written three bestsellers, which would have netted a lot more than that sum.

They claimed he owned an upscale house on the Eastern side of the Volta, but this too was on the word of the man who had built it and allowed Nkrumah to use the facility. Interestingly, Nkrumah had had the Volta dam built below budget and a year ahead of time—a feat unheard of in those or any subsequent times. Both the USA and the USSR had some hand in the overthrow. The Soviets had done a dirty deal on him. Promising not to release any cocoa sold to them by Ghana, they immediately sold a large shipment to Switzerland. One strategy to stop Nkrumah was to reduce the price of cocoa. Ordinary Ghanaians had smuggled the cocoa plant into Ghana in the nineteenth century and by 1960, Ghana was the world's leading exporter of the product. The vast decrease in the price of cocoa saw a drastic decline in the standard of living of many Ghanaians. The USA also thought he was too nationalistic. They involved both the Peace Corps and the CIA in the process. There was distinct dissatisfaction, however, with the regime. Life had become tough, and this afforded the opportunity for the coup d'état. Some of the complaints were justified.

Some necessary food items were in short supply. Nkrumah, who had in his early years been out amongst the people, was forced by the various attempts on his life to stay away from the public spaces. The result of this was that his officers would show him the outskirts of a field, which they would claim was all planted, but which was not planted beyond what he could see from the roadside. Some complaints were nothing short of ridiculous. The people of Southern Ghana because of the tsetse fly of the forest area were unaccustomed to pure milk. They drank milk with their tea or sometimes even drank plain evaporated milk from the Netherlands. Government had replaced this with what tasted like real milk in small tetra packs and people almost rioted for the loss of their Dutch milk!

Interestingly, Nkrumah had had all the plotters against him imprisoned, but executed none of them. When the military and the Police chose to stage a coup while he was out of the country, they made sure that he did not re-enter Ghana. He was forced to live in Guinea with his friend President Sekou Touré. When Nkrumah eventually died in Guinea, there was some hesitation in having his body returned to Ghana for burial. The military junta was afraid of possible repercussions. I wrote an article for the *Barbados Advocate*, predicting that in keeping with West African custom, the Government would eventually allow his body to be interred in Ghana. The newspaper ignored the article and published a similar, but much later European article post facto.

Interestingly, Nkrumah had detained a number of people who were considered as politically dangerous. Most of them were common criminals. The new government decided to release them as a token of their 'legitimacy'. The crime rate in Accra rose astronomically. The peak of this wave came one Fourth of July. Many of the US diplomats lived in one large building. They left for the party with a number of security personnel in charge. A gang came by, well armed and with trucks. They tied up the guards—one was not found until two days later—and cleaned out every apartment of furniture and whatever goodies they could find. It was probably only then that the military recognised that they had released a mob of common criminals.

The legacy of Nkrumah has been phenomenal. Most Ghanaians now realise that they had in this man a giant from a small Akan sub-group, the Nzima. His vision was much wider than they could have imagined. When he helped Southern African Freedom Fighters, he was seen by many to have been wasting their taxes on issues that did not concern them. There would probably not be one Ghanaian who thinks like that today. His vision for Africa is taking some time to materialize, but many see it as inevitable. His contribution to education in Ghana is now paying off in areas of technology, which puts Ghana way ahead of most Caribbean countries. The development plans drawn up by one of the brilliant Ghanaians I had the honour to have studied with at Legon now have that country on the road to becoming a high earning country. There is now an Nkrumah group, which has ensured that his birthday will once again become a national holiday. I am, in that transformation, reminded of a friend of mine at Legon. When he realised that the international student grouping he belonged to was being funded by the CIA, he converted from the most fervent anti-Nkrumah student to one to whom I had difficulty explaining that Nkrumah had made some errors. For him, Nkrumah had made none.

Having finished my Master's in African Studies, I became a little reckless. I forgot all about my prophylactic medicine for malaria and I fell to the disease. I went in to the University hospital and told the doctor, who was a friend, that I needed some quinine tablets to get rid of my mild malaria. He examined me and told me that he was having me admitted to the hospital. I protested that I had my car and could not leave it in the parking lot. "Give me your keys," he said in a voice somewhere between a friendly request and a military command. I surrendered my keys, but protested that I had no pyjamas with me. "That's alright," he continued, "we have a few pairs here that will fit you."

I was accordingly admitted and within an hour my temperature had risen to somewhere near 104 degrees F. I was there for a week, during which I lost 5 pounds even though I had been at my best fighting weight at that time. I was cured and have never had malaria again. But then Ghana had a few excellent hospitals at the time and had pioneered research into sickle cell anaemia as well as having been the third country to successfully perform open-heart surgery.

Before leaving Ghana, I had applied for three different jobs. I wrote the Chief Personnel Officer in Bridgetown and UNESCO in Paris. In the interim, an Atlanta, Georgia University group taking several US students on a West African educational tour asked me to work with them. That was an exciting experience. The Professor later wanted me to come and teach at his University. However, I was off to London.

Within about a month, UNESCO responded. They

kept a conversation going, so I knew they were interested, Finally, I was informed that someone would be coming through London. Could I meet him? I knew that this was a sort of interview they were scheduling, so I prepared myself. I had always been good at interviews, so I did well and they said that they would be in touch with me. I was later offered a choice between a post in Freetown, Sierra Leone and one in a village in Liberia.

Leaving Ghana was like leaving a slice of my heart behind. I had met some formidable characters in my four years there. There was Ayi Kwei Armah, whom I mentioned before. He had the quickest hands I have ever seen. A fly would perch on someone's head and he would say; "Stay still," and with a single swat, that hardly reached beyond the hair, would kill the fly. He was much more than an excellent writer. We had roamed all around Accra to find a tro-tro (minibus) with the title for his first novel painted on the back. I was to do the photograph for the cover of his book. We never found it and I ended up merely doing his photograph for the back cover. The book *The Beautyful Ones Are Not Yet Born* was a brilliant first novel that impelled him to fame as a writer.

And there was the Bajan-Trinidadian, Roy Watts, television producer and later the man in charge of Trinidad TV and Radio. He died in what was pronounced a car accident. Roy told the funniest stories about his life, while being an incredible observer of nature. He had remarked that the beautiful, large Ghanaian lizard did not eat plain white rice. I did not believe him. We were eating at the press club in the open air. There was a lizard below where we were eating and he said: "Watch."

He threw some white rice out and the lizard ignored it. Then he dipped the same rice into what Ghanaians called the soup or we the sauce and threw that out. The lizard gobbled it up. He then proceeded to give a commentary on the fight, which developed between a young male challenger and the older male lizard.

Roy had studied TV in New York. He told a famous story about his first summer there. Needing a job, he applied to be plumbing supervisor at a company that did repairs all over the city. His uncle had been a plumber and Roy certainly knew the terminology of plumbing. So he got the job. However, he knew little about actual plumbing. So he walks on to the floor of the repair shop and asks who was the lead plumber. A little old man whom they called Reds stepped forward. Roy explained that where he came from the foreman oversaw the whole work force but did not actually do any of the plumbing.

After one month, productivity increased. The company offered him a raise. After the second month, it got even better. Roy was by now somewhat more familiar with actual plumbing. They offered him a second raise. Roy declined that in favour of a raise for Reds and a small raise for the other workers. After the end of the third month, Roy had to return to college. Productivity had once more gone up and the company was offering him not only a raise, but also all sorts of incentives to continue. He opted for his TV production career.

There was also Genoud. Roget Genoud was a brilliant Swiss linguist who was the head of the School of Languages. He was one of the most fun-loving persons I have ever met. He loved parties where his friends could discuss any topic, and he invariably joined in. What he however did not like was any German–speaking Swiss national. He spoke German, but that was not the issue. Things came to a head once when we were downtown in a bar. I do not have any idea what the German Swiss said, but Roget attacked him physically and we had to restrain him and get him out of the bar. And he was perfectly sober.

Then there was Ray Kea, who studied with me. He too was a man of considerable ability and also peaceful, except when he was hungry. Then he would rant and rave. He was also one of the few people I have known who were better when they were drunk. He had been a US soldier in Germany, but never spoke a word of German until one night, when he was tipsy and there was a student from Chad. Ray spoke Danish as well, his wife's language but no French. However, to everyone's amazement, Ray conducted an extensive conversation with the scholar and everyone else who understood or spoke German was silent.

When I was about to leave Ghana, Roget had already left, so too had Ray. Only Roy of that trio remained during those dark days of the military. He had some chickens, which he claimed came to him when he called them by the specific name he had given each chicken.

One day, a thief broke into his backyard and stole a few of his chickens. That was when Roy decided that it was time to return to the Caribbean. I was off to London to attempt the impossible. I also remember Roy just before he married his American girlfriend Peggy. When Vernon Smith visited Ghana, we all took a walk on Labadi Beach. Someone decided that it would be a good idea to get some coconut water. I knew I could not climb the tree that stood there daring us to climb it. Roy got up to the point where there was a cluster of coconuts and promptly slid all the way down. Vernon actually reached the nuts, held on to one and then slid all he way down with a single coconut. We decided to pick some mangoes growing further along the beach instead.

The final character of the piece was Wen Su-Tung, a Chinese lecturer of zoology. His family was one of the wealthy families who had fled Mainland China for Taiwan during the period of the Japanese invasion of the Chinese mainland. Su-Tung was not in line with his family's thinking and was also unsure of what would have happened to him under Chairman Mao, so he fled China and ended up in Ghana, then a progressive country under Kwame Nkrumah. He was an expert on West African art and happened once to have a seller come to buy back from him a piece of art he had willingly sold to Dr. Wen. And Su-Tung was a great cook. One night, however, he invited a friend to dinner. They both had the same propensity—falling asleep, and fell asleep they did with the stove still burning. When they woke at three a.m., everything had been burnt, Su-Tung had no more food to cook, and nowhere in town was open.

Those were the normal things about him. Su-Tung had absolutely no sense of direction. He used to come to my apartment, but always accompanied. I did not understand this, since I lived in an apartment visible from the main road from the University into Accra. I did, however, get the full picture when two stories were told to me. There are two roads that lead from the Kwame Nkrumah circle into the centre of Accra. On one of the side roads that connect these two roads, there was a chicken restaurant downstairs and a nightclub directly above in a two-storey building. Su-Tung used to frequent the two places, but always travelling to the restaurant by one road and the nightclub by the other. It took him two years to realise that he went to a single building using two different roads!

As a joke, someone provided him with a mirror image map to a party. He realised almost immediately that he had been given such a map and arrived on his own safely and easily. At such a party, Su-Tung could easily fall asleep amidst the party din, suddenly wake up and say: "My goodness, I have to feed my animals." He was studying nocturnal creatures like the lemur.

His ability to fall asleep was incredible. The instability of his car was legendary. On one occasion when his brakes failed, he found himself driving to the head of a military parade. The officer in charge of the exercise asked: "What have I done to you? Why do you want to get me fired?"

Su-Tung's coup de grace, however, was the result of a

party held in Achimota, a township famous for its school and an area where a number of the University lecturers lived. At this particular party, someone infused a good deal of local distillation into the punchbowl. Several persons left the party drunk. Among these was Su-Tung.

Next day he woke up and found his right front lamp severely battered and could only explain this by claiming to have struck a rock along the Achimota to Legon road. There were no walls or rocks along that road. Su-Tung figured he must have hit something in the gutter. He had on one very sober occasion fallen asleep and driven about two miles with two of his tyres on the road and the other two in the gutter. But there were no rocks there either. Two days later, he noticed an indentation on his garage door, which perfectly matched the damage done to his headlight. Several years later, I met Su-Tung, who was married, had a son and worked in the Ministry of Agriculture. He looked almost as young as he had looked nearly 40 years before.

I will always remember the fellowship I had with these people, and the generous intellectual conversations their company seemed to generate.

England Again

ENGLAND WAS like a wet flower. It seemed to rain all the time. I had returned with the notion of doing a PhD on Scandinavian involvement in the slave trade on the West African coast, but most, if not all of my research material was to be found in the British Museum, which happened to be open at the same time as I had to do supplementary teaching to be able to survive. I therefore ended up spending just under a year there.

Mickey was still in London and in spring he decided that he would do a European trip. I agreed to join him and do some of the driving. He did not come alone. There was a girlfriend, who by the end of the trip was no longer a girlfriend. She talked demeaningly about "lower class people." The sentiment did not appeal to either of us. We drove through Sweden from Gothenburg to Stockholm and then down through Europe. We tried to make it through Denmark and into Holland before nightfall. It was spring and we did not have enough time to do so. We did not wish to run out of gas in the process.

As usual, we could not find a gas station, so we decided to pull off the road and wait until daylight when, almost certainly, any station we found would be open. Mickey slept in the passenger seat, while I slept in the driver's seat and the girlfriend had the back seat all or herself. She snored mightily and was the only one fresh in the morning.

We drove about 200 metres to the next gas station only to discover that it had been open all night! Easter was coming up and we ploughed on to our next stop in The Hague, where a couple, old friends from earlier London days, lived. He was an engineer who had done quite well and she was aspiring to be a sculptor. I was never too fond of her, although Mickey and Vernon had found her charming. They lived in a large penthouse apartment. When we arrived, she informed us that she had booked a couple of rooms for us across the canal. This was passing strange for a West Indian who had more than enough room to accommodate the three of us.

What took the cake was when she invited us along with another couple to an Indonesian restaurant in town and ordered two rijsttafels! A rijsttafel is an Indonesian dish of rice with endless small plates of various meats. One rijstaffel would have been sufficient for the seven of us, but she thought it inappropriate to order only one. The bill, she assured us would be on her husband's entertainment account. However, before the end of the meal she announced that it was time to pass the hat around! She was making us contribute to a meal that would be paid for by her husband's company! Mickey is not a great eater, but he was so angry that he must have eaten half a rijsttafel on his own! He remained angry even when we returned to our lodgings. Instead of sleeping in the room with his girlfriend, he chose to sleep in the extra bed in mine. He soon burst into a fit of invectives over what had happened.

We then drove into Paris, where the girlfriend took a flight back to Canada. It was 1968 and Paris was in student uproar, with Danny the Red and other left wing students, some of whom were to become prominent figures in French politics dominating the scene. I thought it must have been like the uproar of 1848 with Marx and Engels in the forefront. We returned to London with a promise to return to Barbados where we had contributions to make.

In the interim, UNESCO indicated that someone from UNESCO would be in London and wanted to talk to me. I wisely took this to mean an interview. It turned out to be a rather larger group than one and a full interview started. I have always found that the best way to be interviewed is to take the attack to the interviewer. By this I do not mean to suggest that one should attack the interviewer, but that one should as far as possible turn the interview into a general discussion. I had read up on new teaching techniques and I found a good moment to broach the subject. They liked the discussion, which had begun as an interview, and informed me that I would hear from UNESCO soon.

I continued to teach part-time in London, hoping to hear from Barbados. I had decided to skip the possibility of teaching at Morehouse, an Atlanta University, an additional job that was on offer, but I was still interested in a post in Barbados. The Public Service was then as it often is now, silent. UNESCO spoke first. They offered me the possibility of the post of expert, either in Liberia or Sierra Leone. I chose Sierra Leone largely because Milton Margai, where I was to be sent, was a Secondary Teacher Training College just outside Freetown and the Liberian post was of a lower academic standing and somewhere up country, as one says there.

One year after I had applied for a post in the Public Service and somewhat after the concluded UNESCO offer, Barbados replied that they wanted me to join the Mission in London. I was forced to refuse the offer. I proceeded to Paris for the requisite briefing.

Paris, as usual, was interesting. The Algerian War was over, but there was still some ill feeling towards North Africans there. I happened to have been lodged in a hotel near the 'Quartier', and being rather fond of North African food, I often ate there with my North American girlfriend, who had accompanied me to Paris. The greeting to me was invariably warm. I was always addressed as 'frère'. And the couscous was great.

Sierra Leone

WITHIN A few weeks, I was off to Freetown. The flight there on a French airline, UTA, was possibly the worst flight I have ever had. It had little to do with the airline as such, but it was a night flight with a mass of small children who cried and screamed all night. I could not sleep. Arrived at Lungi Airport, we had to take a ferry over the impressive Sierra Leone River to Freetown. That prolonged the agony. When I finally arrived at the Paramount Hotel in Freetown, I climbed into a very comfortable bed. I had managed to sleep for somewhat less than one hour when an overeager officer from the College came to collect me at seven a.m. to take me up to Milton Margai College. I believe it was a Sunday morning as well. I was not to begin a new term for another week.

I was lodged in a house paid for by UNESCO situated right across the road from a pleasant little beach. Oddly, I seldom swam at that beach. I remember once having bought a nearly 100 pound tarpon from someone at that beach. But people who visited me liked the beach and I would naturally join them. The 'real' beaches were further along the peninsula, which formed the Freetown area, with names like Number Two Beach or Sussex Beach etc.

Sierra Leone was a new experience. Although it boasted of being the Athens of West Africa—yes it was a very neo-colonial place—it was now way behind Ghana in practically any area. The Creoles—mainly of Barbadian and Jamaican descent and freed Yoruba taken off slave ships by the British—felt superior to the upcountry people and there was a distinct swagger about them that eventually was to lead to a vicious civil war. Interestingly, the early Creoles who had planted large swathes of citrus fruit up the hills that surround Freetown, no longer bothered with such horticulture. They were now lawyers, teachers, civil servants and the like. The Lebanese had taken over the shops that once were the ground floor of their habitation and were doing well enough to acquire the entire trade that the Creoles had once created and enjoyed.

But I thrived there at this time before the collapse of civil society. The students were keen to learn and I made one great friend on the teaching staff, Logie Wright, the music teacher. Apart from that I frequently limed at the Palm Court, a neat little bar and restaurant, where I acquired friends like Kevin, the Irish banker and Mohammed, a Sierra Leonean engineer, who had studied in Germany. Alex, the Russian-Icelandic keeper of the Court, also became a friend. He, several months later, even joined me on a trip to Barbados.

One night, I walked into the bar and Alex asked me if a bottle of rum he had in his hand was real. It said boldly on its exterior "Alleyne Arthur". I informed him that the only way I could tell was by tasting the contents. So he opened it and it was the real Bajan stuff. I asked how he got hold of the rum. He informed me that he had been in the harbour and met a sailor who needed some money. He was prepared to sacrifice a case of rum for that. I suggested to Alex that he put away two or three bottles for our private usage, but that he could sell the remainder. Even back then, Bajan rum had an enormous appeal.

I believe that it was about two nights later that I returned to taste the brew. Both Kevin and Mohammed, not the fervent Muslim the name might suggest, were there. I told them about the rum and we ordered two bottles. We sipped the brew gently, with the respect due to a spirit less available than a double malt whiskey in Freetown. In the interim, there was a German at the far end of the bar, who had started to fall under the weight of his drinking. Mohammed said that he would begin by moaning, then he would sing and finally he might fall off the barstool. When the first two stages occurred as predicted, we ensured that he did not fall on to the floor.

We, however, continued to sip our brew until the two bottles had, as it were, evaporated. I had had a lift to Palm Court since my car was in the garage. I had to decide who was closer to being sober—Kevin or Mohammed. I decided against driving home with Kevin. He was ranting in French, fortunately not a widely spoken language in Freetown, that if one had not slept with Antoinette, a rather beautiful Guinean woman, one did not know what being with a woman was like. I therefore asked

Mohammed to drop me just beyond the far end of the bay. I arrived home very safely. I was most surprised, however, when I returned to the Palm Court a few days later and found Mohammed. The first question he asked me was how I got home the few nights before!

One of my first extra-mural tasks was to organise a cricket team at the College. I played for this team throughout my stay in Sierra Leone and often played for the Freetown team against the team from the mining sector, Kono, which also had several expats who played the game. I managed to bring along from the College team a student who later became a Member of Parliament. His name was Alfred George. He was a powerfully built young man, with more than a modicum of athletic skills. He could bowl a bit, but lacked the practice of growing up in a cricket environment. He took two catches that amazed me. The first was a skier and the sun was right in his eyes. He took one hand to shade out the sun and caught the ball with the other hand. The second was in a regional match, where he was fielding rather close in at silly mid-on. The batsman smacked the ball really viciously. Nobody quite saw the ball, but it was in Alfred's hand! I even played for the national team against Nigeria. I took five wickets in one innings and scored 42 and 45, but since there was only one other player who reached 40, we were beaten quite easily. I also rather unexpectedly scored a century in my final match, a sort of farewell affair.

Back at my house, I had also been gifted a 'steward' by my predecessor. A steward was a person who ran the household, cooked, washed and ironed etc. It was never a woman. Amadou was from Guinea and was a fabulous cook. He had a wife and a very charming daughter. I seldom saw his wife, but the little daughter often popped up. In fact, the two of them, Amadou and his daughter, appear as characters in my first novel, which was based, although fictitiously, in Sierra Leone.

I also played rugby and came into contact with a fine person, a mining engineer who had studied at Oxford, Tani Pratt. As a result, I met his sister, who was to become my wife and bear me three very interesting children. Only my elder daughter was born in Freetown.

In my early period there, I had many girlfriends. None of them appealed to me as a potential wife.

Then I met Adé, the sister of Tani Pratt, the rugby player. She was quite different from my first wife. She needed nothing in particular. She was from an upper middle class family and was quite comfortable, living up on her hill. I proposed to her and she agreed to marry me. Her parents had no objection to the marriage. Her mother was a Porter with Barbadian ancestry.

Adé and I were married in a little church in Sussex, a tiny village near the sea. It was a rather quaint ceremony with the main speaker preaching at me about money. Soon afterwards, we took off for London and Barbados. I had not been home in thirteen years. My mother was so delighted with my wife that she treated me as if I were the son-in-law. Two years later, when we returned to Barbados with Tanya, our first daughter, Adé found out what it was like to be downgraded. It moved me to third position, but it is a lot easier moving from two to three than it is from first to second.

Back in Freetown, I was part of the UN group in Sierra Leone. One day I was travelling on a bus with one of the UN wives, her sister and her three small children. They sat behind me, chattering away in Swedish. They were talking about me, saying rather flattering things. When they were leaving the bus, I said to the very pretty mother, in Swedish, that she should be careful that the children did not get their fingers caught in the door. It is difficult to describe other people's reactions, but I believe that they would have disappeared from the face of the Earth, if it had been possible.

I cooked on one occasion for my wife's parents. This astounded the mother in particular, but they enjoyed the meal. I also cooked for the Swedish woman and her husband, the Hanssons. They were soon to leave Freetown for another posting in East Africa, but it seemed that we were to remember each other for decades to come. There are some incredible turns in one's life that occur without any real warning.

Adé and I were also part of a scrabble gaggle that took place in different homes across Freetown. We played on Sundays, I believe. We also on one occasion set out to see a part of the country that people from the peninsula seldom ventured into. Before I had met my wife, I did have a girlfriend, who lived in Magburka. So I had visited that small town and crossed a very narrow bridge in dense fog to get back to Freetown on an early Monday morning. But we were venturing much further north, to Kabala.

Kabala is situated in the Sahel, so it is in a rather dry climate. It was December and it was cold. It could not have been higher than 14 degrees Celsius, and Adé froze. But we enjoyed this largely Muslim part of the country with the men all wearing their djellibas and their hats. Women dressed ordinarily, only in much warmer clothing than we had brought.

The road to Kabala was rough, and although not very long, had taken several hours. We therefore thought that it would have been unwise to buy any of the very plentiful beef. Beef in Freetown was from cows, which had walked all the way from the north and was, as to be expected, tough. But we bought two filets to take back with us. They were probably the best filets mignons I have ever had.

I also met a family with a young daughter named Sankoré. This had been the name of the woman who owned the last well coming from North Africa into Timbuktu as well as the famous university in that city. We agreed then that we would name our first daughter Sankoré. So we did name our first daughter Tanya Sankoré. She was a delightful child. She had to be woken up at night to be fed. What was more astounding was that she would sleep through the sound and light fury, which gave the country its name.

Evidently, the European captain who first came to

Sierra Leone was Italian, so he named the country Sierra (mountain in Spanish) and Leone (lion in Italian). This was because of the wild lightning and thunderstorms, which occurred before the mid-year rains. The noise from the thunder roared throughout the ring of mountains that surround the capital area. Lightning that flashed through the entire apartment invariably preceded this. This would also wake Adé and me up, but never bother Tanya.

Her mother, an academic, had read everything about childcare and therefore fed her as the books suggested appropriate.

We took Tanya to some ten different countries before she was two. One of the first countries was Sweden. Tanya was completely confused by the Swedish summer. I had had a basketball accident while in Ghana. While there had been doctors who could do the operation to remove my shattered minisci, they did not have the equipment to conduct the operation, so I waited until I could get back to Sweden. Tanya and her mother joined me there. In a Stockholm summer, the sun comes up at about 2.30 a.m. and it does not get dark until 11 pm. We had to explain to Tanya that it was bedtime; even though the sun was still in the sky or that it was not yet time to wake up. She seemed to understand since she would go to bed or return to bed as the case might be.

Tanya was probably the most delightfully obedient and pleasant child I have ever known. She had to be woken up to be fed even when she was only days old. We had a bookshelf that came all the way down to the floor with books. I told Tanya that books were precious and that she should not interfere with our books, since she had five of her own. She would walk around with her five books more like any other child would walk around with a doll or teddy bear and ambush any visitor with: "Tell me a story" or "Well then read a story to me."

Even when she was much older and at a somewhat racist school in Washington DC, I used to pick her up at school closing time except when I was out of the office or otherwise occupied with work that I could not leave. On such occasions, Nestor the office driver would pick her up and bring her to the office. The horrible woman who was office manager waited till one day when I was at a meeting with Ambassador Jackman and ensured that Nestor could not pick her up. When I returned and did not find Tanya, I asked the office manager where she was. She replied: "I do not have any children."

I rushed off to the school. It was winter and it was already dark. There was no one left at the school. It was nearly five p.m. There she was on the dark path outside the school, singing. I apologised for being so late. She simply said: "That's alright. I knew you would come for me." I nearly cried.

One day back at Milton Margai, I ran into Stokely Carmichael, who had once even terrified the Government of Barbados into removing the freedom of association clause from the rights Barbadians could claim in the Constitution. He was now Kwame Touré. We chatted briefly about music, but he seemed to be nothing as fiery as he used to be in former times. Another Milton Margai moment was when I invited an officer from the US Embassy to speak to the History Club. I believe his talk was focused on democracy. One of the students asked him bluntly why the USA had been on the wrong side in Vietnam. No one expected such a question and the officer mumbled some response. After the session, one of the students thanked him for having spoken.

The students at Milton Margai were quite an interesting lot. The President of the History Club was a Physics student! There was also another UNESCO expert in Education from Australia. At first, the students complained that they could not understand him, but after a few weeks, they were all imitating his Australian accent and speech. And then there was the concert. A German student orchestra came to the College to play for the students. Unexpectedly, they played all modern classical European music, which was cacophonous. The students loved it and embraced the German students almost as brothers.

The students were what I missed most about Sierra Leone. Sierra Leone was a study in itself. This magnificent country with mountains that roared like lions and then found themselves covered by bright flashing lightning, this country of mountainous territory surrounding the Freetown area itself, had once been the place of refuge for Barbadians and Jamaicans who had fought with the British in North America. They were later to be joined by Nigerians taken off non-British slave boats after Britain had abolished the slave trade. They all settled in the area around Freetown. My Sierra Leonean wife had a Bajan great-grandfather with the name Porter.

Even then the upcountry vs. Creole division was beginning to manifest itself in minor conflicts. It did not help that corruption at the highest level had increased. Siaka Stevens, who had been elected Prime Minister in 1967, had mixed Creoles with upcountry folk in his Parliament. He was not Creole himself, but had grown up and gone to school in Freetown. His action eased the tension. However, Mr. Stevens was irreparably corrupt. After he had converted the country to a Republic, he became the President. After Stevens' death, the divide became once again very heated, leading to the massacres and limb-cutting which characterised a more recent part of that country's history.

Then there was the incident where a plane loaded with some 18 million pounds sterling worth of diamonds flew from Kono to Wellington, a small airport outside Freetown. The diamonds disappeared and someone had to be charged. A Lebanese merchant evidently called the best lawyer in town late at night. On arriving, the lawyer said: "A quarter million pounds! Now what is it?" He knew that anyone calling him that late at night was in serious trouble. There was a half-Lebanese also involved, but he seemed to have been the President's man and he did not have to run like the merchant.

Things got worse and there was an attempted coup. I was on my way into Freetown, when someone shouted to me "A coup!" I turned around and drove at a speed of 70 miles per hour out of town. I only stopped when a soldier, manning one of the military blockades, stopped me. "Open your trunk!' he said. I explained that I was UN staff and… "Open your trunk!" he repeated more fiercely. I complied. Diplomatic immunity means nothing to an angry soldier with a loaded rifle.

My neighbour endured one harrowing, though hilarious, incident from the coup. He worked for the Ghana Embassy in downtown Freetown. His lunch was usually two sausage rolls and a drink of some sort. He reached home that day about four o'clock and I met him on the stairway. He said he had just bought his sausage rolls when armed soldiers entered the hotel. Like everyone else he got onto the floor and crawled under the table. "In the process" he said, "I lost my sausage rolls and I am so hungry."

The coup failed and Stevens continued on his corrupt way until he retired from politics in the nineteen eighties. He then appointed an army officer as President. It is said that when he was on his deathbed, his children sat around him and each time he coughed they leaned closer to hear the number of his so secret Swiss bank account. He never revealed it.

There were some beautiful things about Sierra Leone, but these were in the area of ordinary people or the physical country itself. The rainy season was a magnificent spectacle. It could rain up to 6 inches in successive days. The deep gutters in the city provided the necessary runoff, so I do not ever remember flooding in the city. Additionally the main road in the city sloped downward to the River, so water disappeared almost as soon as it fell. However, the mountains just outside the city limits were different. During the rains, springs would pop up all over the mountainside. It was a magnificent sight. However, throughout this period, the humidity was at 100% and clothes would not dry. They had to be ironed just before wearing.

The Creoles were occasionally none too pleasant. Sierra Leone is a tropical country and there is plenty of African clothing that can be considered formal. However, Sierra Leonean Creole men, like Bajan lawyers always wore black suits both at night and in the middle of the hot day. I wondered if they had reprogrammed their sweat glands. I simply wore what we call shirt jack suits.

Then one day a West Indian who had lived there for quite a while came to me and said that he noticed that I always wore yumma yumma clothing to people's soirées. I pointed out that I believed that he was carrying a message and I did not want to shoot the messenger, so I suggested that the persons who had invited me to their parties wanted to have me there. If they did not like my choice of clothing, please let them know that I would not be offended if they did not invite me. The invitations, however, never stopped.

Sierra Leone could have become one of the more developed countries on the African Continent, if only it had been blessed with proper leadership. The first Finance

Minister of Siaka Stevens suggested that Stevens should use monies from the rich diamond fields to develop the country. There was the possibility of creating a dam on the Sierra Leone River near Magburka that would have provided electricity for the entire country as well as storing water for an area, which could have become the breadbasket of the country. Mr. Stevens said no. He would borrow money instead. His Finance Minister left. He was more fortunate than some of those who later opposed Stevens and lost their lives.

Oddly, the country is one of the richest in terms of subsoil to be found anywhere. It has gold, diamonds, extremely rich iron ore, rutile etc., all of which have been exploited by foreign countries with precious little return to Sierra Leone. In the earliest years, the Creoles of Freetown had created enormous citrus orchards along the mountainsides and had built West Indian style houses with shops downstairs and living quarters upstairs. But their children became schoolteachers, lawyers and civil servants and sold their businesses to the new Lebanese population. The Creoles then became a largely effete presence in the country that looked down on upcountry folk. My father-in-law for instance had been the head teacher at Ahmadu Jah's school and had always tried to persuade him that as an upcountry boy education was being wasted on him. Creoles talked about Freetown being the Athens of West Africa, their focus always being on Britain and Europe.

When we left Sierra Leone, we went to New York, where a Swede I had met suggested that I would make a good UNDP Representative. He was impressed with my language and people skills particularly. However, he was on his way out and the new man I met insisted that anyone doing the job needed a degree in business or economics, neither of which I then possessed.

Cote D'Ivoire

IT WAS Ama Ata Aidoo, my Ghanaian sister and a writer, who informed me of some US organisation wanting to set up a pre-university school in Ivory Coast for both US, and Ivorian students. They needed someone to run the school and also someone to teach the US students French and the Ivorians English. Adé had a degree in French and Spanish and spoke both languages fluently. We took the job. We had a briefing with the US students and one teacher in the US before setting off for Cote d'Ivoire. That teacher managed to lose the equipment one of the students was carrying for his asthma. The teacher simply lost it. However, marvellously, the student, after two injections at the local Ivoirian hospital, never needed his asthma equipment or medicine again. That student was a young African American who was particularly helpful and always hung around. He would play with Tanya Sankoré, our little daughter, as did all the students. She became the group mascot.

Tanya sang a lot and enjoyed most being in her little basin of water. If she felt miserable as children often do, putting her in the basin full of water changed the world. Interestingly, because of the milieu she was in, French became her first language. We had agreed that one of us should speak French to her and the other English. We were not completely faithful to this arrangement, largely because people who speak several languages have a habit of speaking whatever language is being spoken at the moment. Anyway, Tanya's proclivity for the French language occurred as a fifteen month old when we were driving across the swing bridge in Bridgetown and she saw the water of the careenage and said: "L'eau!" Quickly I replied, "Dirty water." She continued "L'eau—dirty water." I had to correct that to l'eau sale, before the surprising conversation ended.

Bouaké, the Ivory Coast's second town, was quite a revelation. There were some 700 Normans there who played petanque, a variant of boules, on the sidewalks of the street. It was 400 kms from the capital Abidjan. It was however controlled by a mayor from what was then Upper Volta, now Burkina Faso, who was both corrupt and effectively guarding the interests of Ivorian President, Houphet Boigny (Akan: Ofei Boahene). The Mayor was the one to whom we went for small favours. Quite quickly we learnt that white Frenchmen had access to the Mayor before the likes of us. Adé and I both spoke French, but the French of someone from France came with the possibility of a kick back. We had nothing to offer. But the white American kids knew how to play the system. Two of them would dress nicely and go into the supermarket and take whatever they fancied and walk out with it.

According to the general belief, only black people stole

stuff from a supermarket. They would then share whatever goodies they had stolen with the rest of the group. I learnt about all this much later. In any case we lived so close to the poverty line that I could hardly blame them.

We were housed in two small buildings of the Mairie. The US teacher slept in the building with the students and Adé, Tanya and I slept in the smaller building. Sometimes, the monies to support us came late and we would have to survive on atcheké, a local couscous made from cassava. The US kids did not much like this, but Mark, who had grown out of his asthma, had an incredible appetite for someone who was so skinny. So he would eat whatever was left over by the other students.

Mark's appetite was historic. One of his Ivorian friends took him to his village. Twelve of the mothers of the village immediately adopted him and said they would cook for him. It must be understood that what each cooked was the equivalent of what a cane cutter would eat for his midday meal. Mark ate it all, in spite of the warning from his friend and for the first time brought some of it back up. Next time he was offered food from only four mothers and consumed it with no ill effects whatever. Once I invited Mark to the village next to the Mairie for a meal of agouti and atcheké. We sat and ate what was a very large meal. Immediately afterwards, Mark remembered that his Ivorian girlfriend had promised to cook for him. So he hurried home and ate one of those containers one took to the cane fields, full of food. I have seen Mark several times since that sojourn. He is married to a Trinidadian, has worked on Capitol Hill, has a couple of children and is slim as ever. It simply is not fair.

I travelled once to Ghana with Mark. The road was flooded and we had to cross what was in effect a small river. We then took mini-buses all the way to Accra. We must have travelled close to twenty-four hours. Mark slept as if he were in a bed. Arrived, I went to visit my old friend, Kwame Akpini. Kwame was one of the most skilled mechanics I have ever met. We went to his workplace. He indicated that right after work he had to go upcountry to the funeral of the brother of a friend. We could come along.

I was glad we did. Mark got to see an aspect of African life that we would never have observed in Bouaké. African funerals are celebrations of the life of the deceased. So we found ourselves in an open courtyard with lots of people eating and drinking. Then the brother of the deceased came up to us and said: "You have honoured me by coming to the funeral of my brother, but I did not even greet you and ask you if you have had anything to eat or drink." I believe Mark thought that he had come to eject us from the courtyard. In the US we would probably have been ejected; in Barbados even if we were not ejected we would probably have been subjected to a reprimand for being where we were not wanted.

Back in Bouaké, the Mayor informed us that he needed the space we occupied, but that if we could build a structure, he would offer us a bit of land outside the town. So we went out to his farm. I designed a school, and together with the help of a carpenter/mason, we built it. There were two good things that came from this: we were on a farm and had access to some fantastic mangoes and bananas. I even made a concoction I called banango juice. It was well received. It taught us how to build and how to work together. I also had to drive a truck on the farm.

However, soon after we had finished building, the semester ended and we were informed that the company could no longer sustain the school. We were all flown back to New York. I lost touch with most of the students. One of the Ivorians became an actor and worked in some French films, another was pursuing a Ph.D. at Columbia University, and Mark obtained a Master's in Political Science. Very few of the Americans learnt any French, but the Ivorians learnt quite a bit of English and little Tanya left with French as her first language and has never lost it altogether.

While in Bouaké, I met Colin Granderson, a Trinidadian with Bajan roots. He was teaching at a school there. We exchanged details and interestingly, he too later went to Ghana to do the Masters in African Studies. Evidently, he and a group of other teachers were planning a December visit to Timbuktu. I opted in. I could not take Adé and Tanya, but I would only be missed for a fortnight. The trip to Mopti, a town in lower Mali on the Niger River was uneventful. From there we took a boat up river to Timbuktu. The boat ride was much more fascinating. It was on the widest segment of that great river. We could sometimes see no land except for small islets in the stream. We travelled as a group in second class. First class was taken largely by a group of German tourists who were quite obnoxious. As it is cold in Mali at that time of the year, we would go out in the morning and sit on the eastern side of the boat to get warm. The Germans would come down to the second-class deck and walk around, making us draw in our legs to let them pass. They could evidently not walk around on their own deck. Additionally, when we came to a small landing site, they threw bananas into the water for local children to retrieve. I also had later at the hotel to tell one of them off when she tried to commandeer a waiter who was serving a small group of us. She felt it was more urgent that he served her first! I made sure that she understood my reprimand by speaking to her in German.

Otherwise, the boat trip was very enjoyable. In steerage were the ordinary Malians along with one young Swede, who slept on the open deck without a blanket or other cover apart from his shirt and trousers. There were also two incredible musicians, one a blind singer, the other playing a two-stringed guitar. It was a sad music reminiscent of the tone of the descendant music from the Iberian Peninsula, flamenco and fado.

Timbuktu was an unforgettable experience. I met a small group who were the descendants of the Moroccan invaders of 1591. I also visited the Grand Mosque, which had been the site of the Sankoré University long before such institutions had existed in Europe. One had to take off one's sandals and the sand was cold. This great architectural feat had been the work of the re-designer of the city, Es Saheli, who had made the streets run so that the wind would sweep its dust and small debris into the River, which at that time came right up to the edges of the city. (When I visited, the city was some 6 kilometres away. It is probably considerably farther now.)

The prickly pear architecture of Es Saheli found its way eastwards to Djenne as well as southwards through Burkina Faso as far as North-western Ghana. Shafts are built into the adobe structure, making it easy for workmen to climb up the elaborate building to repair any part of the surface, which was crumbling or in need of simple repair.

Much of the rest of the city consists of small flat-roofed houses, many of which are enormous libraries. Many of them are filled with manuscripts that detail a history that we do not yet know and that will undoubtedly shed bright light not only on Timbuktu itself, but also on the history of the entire area of the Sahel.

There was one weird incident of the journey. One night, I went to bed naked and had this strange dream of being terribly frightened. I awoke trembling. I was freezing. I had forgotten that the temperature could fall from daytime highs of 40 Celsius down to 12. I immediately put on a T-shirt, shorts and socks and ran around the room several times before becoming warm again. I returned to bed, removing only my socks and had no more dreams.

The road back was more eventful than the entry. I returned using the ubiquitous mammy lorry (ZR mini-van) and arrived at the Upper Volta border too late to cross over. So had a number of other travellers. A man who lived on the Malian side of the border invited us into his backyard and gave us each a blanket. Even with the blanket, it was none too easy to sleep, since the blanket had to be placed on the ground. It was even colder than in the hotel. I eventually arrived back in Bouaké with a roll of super 8 film and beautiful memories of a city mistakenly believed to be at the back of nowhere.

Back in Barbados

ADÉ, TANYA and I returned to independent Barbados and rented a small chattel house in Britton's Hill, not far from where my mother and stepfather lived. My mother adored little Tanya. She was particularly fond of climbing. At 15 months, she could climb out of her crib by putting one foot to the top of the crib and pulling herself up and then doing a free fall backwards on to the floor. I nearly died when I saw her do this. I wanted to find out how she always got into our bedroom early in the morning.

She could fall asleep on a plank and not fall off. So one day when Mom was driving her in the car and looked back, she could see no Tanya. She got out of the car and there was Tanya fast asleep on the ledge below the rear glass.

And Tanya, just about 15 months old, began to talk. One morning she came in, put her arms around my neck and said: "Hello, baby!" That woke me up. Then for the second time in her little life, she began crying one night. I went to see what was wrong. She was never awake at night not even when the lightning and thunderstorms ripped through our apartment just outside Freetown. I said: "What is the matter, darling?"

141

She replied "Earring biting you."

She was so accustomed to being spoken to as "you" that she thought she was "you." Anyhow, I examined the assaulting earring to find that it was stuck in her nightdress. I dislodged it. She went straight back to sleep. From that moment on, English became her everyday language. By the time she was 2½, she was using words like "actually". I was also amazed at how many things she picked up from simply hearing us speak or at looking at photographs. We took her to a ceremony where the Prime Minister, Errol Barrow was opening a factory or some place of business. Little Tanya patted my leg and said: "Daddy, is that the Prime Minister?"

But she had not forgotten her French. One day about 6 years later, she stormed into our kitchen in Kensington, Maryland and burst into a French soliloquy on what her young sister had done. Her very bright and mischievous sister, Aderonké, followed with "So what have I done now?" Ronké remained monolingual, while Tanya much later added Spanish to her language list, one behind her mother, who apart from speaking excellent French and Spanish, which she had studied at University, also spoke her native Krio.

Adé found a job immediately teaching at Combermere. It took me a while before I was asked to work in a temporary position at the Ministry of Education. There were two great persons at the Ministry at the time. One was a brilliant educator, Rudolph Greenidge and the other was an excellent administrator, Rolf (Frankie)

Jordan. The only thing to be said for the rest was that they would fit admirably in today's dysfunctional public service. Regrettably, I can only recall the nonsense I had to endure with the Education Officers in the Ministry. The first case was the very talented Stewart twin brothers. They had been living in Trinidad, returned to Barbados after third form and proceeded to study on their own for 'O' Levels. In the interim, since they were artists, they decided to open their yard to other kids interested in painting. They ended up after two years with 8 'O' levels each. They then proceeded to study for 'A' levels, at that time a prerequisite for entering University. One twin got back two 'A' levels, the other got three. The better qualified entered for a scholarship in veterinary medicine being offered in Mexico, but the Education Officer said that he was not impressed by the young man's qualifications!

The same officer came up again, when Venezuela offered a 13-month MA course in multiple education fields. I proposed that we could take one Spanish teacher at a time. His response was short, but not sweet: "Our system of education does not mesh with that of the Latins." On another occasion there was a rather long Spanish document. Everyone claimed total unfamiliarity with the language. It ended up on my desk and I ventured a free translation. This led some superior idiot to write the comment: "This is a very free translation."

One other incident involved the Ministry of Finance. Europe had offered us a number of scholarships. There was a deadline of three weeks. I reminded the office in

Finance of this. His reply was that it would take six weeks to process any scholarship and that the Europeans had better understand that. Talk about beggars being choosers!

Foreign Affairs

I WAS not unhappy when Foreign Affairs indicated that they had a vacancy and invited me to apply for it. I did and began a long career in the Foreign Service. One of the very first pleasant moments was when I was part of a small group to meet and entertain the famous Cuban poet, Nicolas Guillen. I remember that our Spanish speaker at that time was Sonja Welch. What was remarkable was that we took Señor Guillen to the Creole restaurant, where we had a delightful eddo soup. He wanted to know what eddo was in Spanish, but no one in the group knew the Spanish equivalent. It was all however, a very pleasant outing.

I found myself in matters of CARICOM quite soon. It was the early seventies and there were two crises. The first one worked in our favour. There was a shortage of sugar on the world market and sugar prices went sky high. Sensibly, I thought, we made an arrangement with the UK to sell sugar at a reasonable price for an extended period. This ended up being the basis of the ACP Sugar Protocol. This in itself was the result of protracted meetings within CARICOM at official as well as at ministerial levels. I was the Foreign Ministry officer responsible for this area, so I often found myself in Georgetown, which at that time was a pleasant place with clean, flowing canals.

I distinctly remember one meeting there, when against my advice to leave Barbados on the Saturday night, the team leader, the Permanent Secretary in the Ministry of Trade, opted for leaving on Sunday. We arrived very late that night and began at nine a.m. later that day. I was immediately put on the regional subcommittee dealing with sugar, so bedtime was at 3.a.m.! The second night ended at 11 pm. The Committee had worked out a very reasonable distribution of sugar quotas between the producing countries. The Ministers wanted to make a political input, so the proposed quota system was thrown out until, after they had argued themselves silly, the great Secretary General, William Demas, re-introduced the same quota we had arrived at official level as a consensus. Everyone was too tired, so they agreed.

The second was the oil crisis where the price of gasoline skyrocketed and shortages occurred. I had to attend the Barbados meetings of Regional leaders on the crisis. One of the things I remember about these meetings was how gentle Prime Ministers Barrow and Manley were to their staff. Burnham, on the other hand once snarled at his Ambassador "You want the work?" an obvious threat to fire him if necessary. This was like Eric Gairy cursing his Permanent Secretary for not having secured an interview for him with a Canadian TV station, while they had asked our Prime Minister to do an interview with them.

However, after only a year in Foreign Affairs, the

Minister of Trade, under whom I worked on CARICOM issues, asked to borrow me to set up an Export Division in the Barbados Investment and Development Corporation. It was great having to report only to my boss, who happened to be my cousin, Rawle Chase, and to the Board that governed the Division. I had only a secretary, Heather Marshall, who was one of the two best secretaries I have ever had. We managed to compile an export directory, which I noticed had not substantially changed several years later.

We also arranged and held a seminar for Barbadian exporters to understand the documentation needed to establish the eligibility of their export goods. She sent out all the invitations, letters to presenters at the seminar and received both the attendees at the seminar as well as their fees. The Hilton venue was packed and the seminar was very well received. Heather had been so effective that I took her out to a steak dinner immediately afterwards as a reward for her excellent service. Interestingly, about one week later, the wife of an old schoolmate, who was responsible for her company's export documentation, called me to say that the old fellow who had attended the seminar instead of her did not seem to understand the process, but had attended the seminar because of seniority. Could I please explain the processes to her so that they could function in the CARICOM market?

I also became helpful to a young Barbadian who came in and announced that he wanted to export fish. We talked about capitalization, ethnic markets and he was off and running. He became one of the biggest and most successful in the business. He never forgot me. Much later when I was in Brussels and wanted to cook Bajan food for my colleagues, I asked the Permanent Secretary in Trade to bring me some flying fish. He went to the same not-so-young man then and said he wanted some fish for the Ambassador in Brussels. He asked the PS for my name. Then he said to the PS: "He can't buy fish from me." He gave him a box of about 6-8 cubic feet full of flying fish.

I attended an export seminar held in Cali, Columbia. I had been in Bogotá before. That had been a very interesting experience in that I had not visited a city of such elevation. I woke up in the middle of the night, breathing erratically. I was not absorbing as much oxygen as I needed. After some deep breathing, I was asleep again. I was warned about pickpockets in Bogotá. So I kept my money and passport well hidden. One day, however, I bought a leather wallet for my brother and casually put it in my coat pocket. Less than fifteen minutes later, the wallet had disappeared.

Cali was different. I arrived at the hotel with two colleagues from Venezuela and Jamaica. It was late afternoon and someone suggested that we should go into town. We were told that it was not far. Without checking on the direction, I opined that the town centre was in a specific direction. Normally, I have a very poor sense of direction. On this occasion, I was totally correct. Arrived there, I sensed that people were standing round and that there was too quiet a scene to be normal. I accordingly advised my colleagues; we returned briskly to the hotel. Not long after, there was a clash between students and the police just about where we had been standing!

The seminar was useful, but I missed one whole morning of it. At the reception the evening before, I ate some shrimps, which made me spend the entire morning in the bathroom. Fortunately, my Venezuelan colleague came by and I got him to bring me some kaopectate. I was functioning again by afternoon, if a little weak. All the other colleagues at the seminar thought that I had had too much to drink the night before and had to wait out a hangover.

○

Soon after that, Foreign Affairs aborted the loan to the BIDC and sent me off to the Embassy in Washington. That was to be the beginning of several miserable years in my life. Almost as soon as I had arrived and was settling in, there was a change of Government in Barbados. The year was 1976, a generally eventful year in the history of Barbados. The DLP Government headed by Errol Barrow suffered its first defeat partly because they had been in office for three five-year terms and partly because of a scandal involving a scientist named Bull, who had evidently been hired by the US and Canada to build a gun, which could fire rockets deep into the stratosphere. Mr. Bull had evidently decided to sell his discoveries to the highest bidder or bidders, who happened to be Iraq and South Africa. Mr. Bull was assassinated in the streets of Brussels fourteen years later. I happened at the time to have known his secretary, who had no clue as to why he had been killed. But then the Mossad in particular or the CIA or the KGB did not leave calling cards after such a deed.

One other incident occurred on the changeover of Government. A Cuban plane, flying from South America with students from Guyana and Korea along with a cadre of Cuban athletes who had competed in Venezuela, was brought down just off the West Coast of Barbados. Orlando Bosch had planted a bomb on the plane, had himself deplaned in Barbados possibly to watch the plane fall from the sky. There were no survivors. Bosch was later freed in the USA—evidently terror against Cuba was not an offence—until his natural death in 2011. He also had the distinction of collaborating with President Reagan and Noriega in a drug selling scheme which provided funding for the Contras.

Washington DC & New York

BACK IN Washington DC, the Ambassador, a member of the losing DLP Party, was recalled with indecent haste. Soon after the Counsellor was called back to Barbados, I was left in charge of the Embassy. The local staff members were abysmal. They expected me to sit behind a desk and not attend meetings of the OAS or visit Capitol Hill. They also expected me to attend every function the local Barbadian community hosted. I had a different vision of my duty.

I also one day caught a member of the same staff copulating with someone in a small, furnished room in the Embassy. He claimed that it was not what I thought I had seen. It was there that the plot was probably hatched. Included in the plot was the Trinidadian chauffeur, who would have been party to the anonymous letter that was cooked up and sent to the Permanent Secretary. It alleged that I often took the official car to a motel. The Trinidadian later told me that it was the car of the Bahamian Embassy, whose driver lived next door! They claimed that I used the official car to buy half a cow and then had most of it hang outside the vehicle; that I harassed the females who came to the Embassy; and that I liked Africans more than Barbadians. To my surprise, the Permanent Secretary wrote me informing me that the Minister wanted to have me respond to the various allegations.

I indicated that I was not aware that one had to respond to an anonymous letter, but since the Minister so insisted, I would. The letter had been signed "Student from Howard (University)." I answered everything in detail. Among other things, my family had not yet arrived in Washington and I lived in a big house in Maryland: why would I go to a motel? The accusation about the cow was equally false, since I took the messenger's car with the messenger himself driving. He was clearly the source of that misinformation as well as the bit about my liking Africans better. A former Ghanaian student had informed me that one could buy meat in bulk at a place in Maryland and he accompanied us. I bought about twenty pounds of beef, which fitted easily into the trunk of the car.

In spite of my clear denial of being guilty of any of the charges—the PS and Minister were both lawyers—I was to be recalled. It was the Barbados UN Representative, Dr. Don Blackman, who stepped in.

He said he wanted me at the UN. So I was hurriedly transferred from Washington to New York. I had been in Washington for a year and Tanya had been sent to a school, which she liked. Her sister, Ronké, born just after the Foreman-Ali fight in Kinshasa, was too young to go to school. We were worried about telling Tanya that we had to leave Washington, but knew that we had to. When we did, Tanya very calmly replied: "I did not know what it would be like when we came here, but I liked it, so we can try New York. Maybe I will like New York too." That was so refreshingly mature that we were confounded.

We were lodged in a hotel in Manhattan for the first month in New York. Tani, Adé's brother, arrived in New York on his way to Philadelphia. Fortunately for him, there was a cricket match scheduled for one of his days staying with us. The former West Indian players were in great number in one of the two teams. Everton Weekes was manager-coach and players included Wes Hall, Garry Sobers, Charlie Griffith, Seymour Nurse et al. Tani who had never seen the greats play was delighted to see Garry score a fifty and wondered whether we could invite them over. I did. They all turned up to dinner in our suite at the hotel, except Charlie Griffith and Everton Weekes. So he actually got to meet most of the old greats.

They were hilarious. Of course they made fun of Charlie in his absence. According to a Seymour Nurse story, they were on the subway. Someone had said to them not to talk to anyone on the subway: it could be dangerous. In came a sturdy, tall black man who mumbled "I gotta get me some money today." Charlie is supposed to have shied away from him. When they got off the train, the man also alit. He turned to Charlie to ask what time it was. According to Seymour, Charlie ran 100 yards down the street and shouted back: "Half past three!" It was a great little dinner party.

We moved to Roosevelt Island situated on the East

River, flowing between Manhattan and Queens. From the living room window of the apartment, we could hear the interminable noise of traffic on the other side of the River. Fortunately, our bedroom window faced the tiny Main Street of the island. The islet, in spite of its many pigeons, was clean, unlike much of New York. A handful of people working at the United Nations, just across the East River lived there. Kofi Annan and the late Felix Downes-Thomas lived there. They were both friends. The most senior of the US Fifth Committee members also lived there.

My indelible memory of New York was the winter of 1978-9. Folk had walked their dogs, which had defecated on the streets. The snow came and covered it over. This happened maybe three times that winter. When April of the latter year came and all the snow melted, the three layers of dog faeces re-emerged with the most horrendous of smells. The mayor almost immediately passed his pooper-scooper law, requiring all who walked dogs to carry with them a bag and a scooper so as to avoid any such occurrence ever again.

New York was good for my career, as it was good for Tanya. She was enrolled at the UN School, where she did gymnastics. One of her colleagues—he was a much better gymnast—was Pele's son. I became involved in the parent teacher meetings and they elected me to the Board of the school. My younger daughter, Aderonké, was also quite happy. She went to a school near the UN building and turned out to be one of the brightest children in the school/kindergarten. When we had to leave New York, again quite suddenly, the school offered to give her a scholarship if she could stay on. My wife Adé got an OAS scholarship and enrolled at Columbia to do a Master's in Educational Psychology. She had always claimed that she needed to sleep for 10 hours a day, but throughout that period, she never slept for more than four hours each night, she played hostess to my colleagues and studied most of the rest of the time. We had brought a helper, Avril from Barbados and she took care of the children. Adé too was very happy.

One incident I recall from fairly early in my stint in New York was orchestrated by a man I considered a friend; we often played bridge together. He took me to a restaurant where I was supposed to meet someone whom I suspected would have been a CIA agent. It turned out to be a gentleman who spoke with an Austrian or Germanic accent. It was obviously recognised that I knew Ambassador Salim Ahmed Salim and possibly other African Ambassadors. Salim Ahmed Salim was running against Kurt Waldheim, an alleged earlier Nazi, for the post of UN Secretary General. The USA did not want the former to win, since ujamaa of Tanzania was considered a form of Communism. The 'Austrian' gentleman wanted me to provide dirt on any or many African Ambassadors. I would be paid handsomely. He could also ensure, he claimed, that I would be rapidly promoted within the Barbados system. I walked away. I do not recall ever seeing my friend again.

I found myself in the Fifth Committee, which scrutinised the budget and administration of the UN system. Within a year I was elected Vice-Chairman of the Committee, which meant that I had to chair some meetings. On such occasions, David Blackman, an accountant who worked in the Consulate General, sat in the Barbados seat. I remember two fascinating stories about him. I asked him to prepare a response to the Budget that had been presented. He did. I then informed him that I would sit behind him and he would present the Barbados statement. He was excellent. On another occasion when I was in the Chair, there was a dispute about the provision of a Secretary on the Committee set up to promote the independence of Namibia. The hardliners wanted a new secretary; the British, USA and the USSR did not want to spend any money on new staff. The UN came up with a solution. They would provide a secretary from elsewhere in the system. I called one of the attendants and gave her a note for David, which said: "Say yes, but say no."

He understood and explained that while Barbados was in favour of a completely new secretary, we would be willing to accept the UN proposal. That became the consensus.

We worked long hours in the Fifth. It was actually not all tedium. John, the man who operated the speaking system, offered to bring the mixers and we—the other vice-chairmen of the Committee—would provide the harder stuff. It took the edge, as they say, off the long days and nights. I also made friends with several of my colleagues. The Ethiopian who sat behind me proudly informed me that he had had a Barbadian teacher in his first school. And there was the Portuguese female representative, the Ghanaian, the Indian and the Caribbean representatives who were invariably helpful. The Portuguese colleague had fallen under the charms of my daughter, Tanya. Invited to a reception at the Indian representative, I asked if I could bring along Tanya since her mother Adé was indisposed. I was informed that they had a son of the same age and that it was fine. Tanya was delighted. The son shyly disappeared from the scene, but Tanya said to the hostess "I do not know anything about making drinks, but I could help you take them to the various guests." And she did. One went to the Portuguese delegate, who was blown away by this very little girl with all that poise. From then on, whatever I proposed, I could count on a Portuguese vote.

I did propose a thing or two. One Resolution was for the hiring and promotion of more women and persons from developing countries. Some of my colleagues suggested that it would not pass. Determined, I enlisted all the help I could. I contacted every female delegate. I also went to the Norwegian candidate and said, speaking in Swedish, that since they were so keen on gender equality I would expect them to vote with me. Finally (the idea for the resolution had come from Barbados with a bit of nudging) on an occasion when the Minister visited New York, I had him call in about 70 Ambassadors in one day.

Opposition to the idea came from the Secretary General,

Kurt Waldheim, who is reported to have said something about those troublesome 'fifth' secretaries, an intended insult since there was nothing that mathematically high. He was ably supported by one of the Central American Ambassadors. The Brazilian Chargé d'Affaires informed me that he was sympathetic, but would not confront another Latin Ambassador. However, when it came to a vote, he would vote yes. All the female delegates, with the exception of the Somali representative, voted in favour of the resolution. I had also canvassed the Eastern European delegates. Ambassador Fokine of the USSR and I used to exchange Barbados rum for Russian wines and vodka at Xmas and the Hungarian delegate was a friend. The Resolution passed relatively easily. I had touched the liberal nerve of most of the delegations. Waldheim was defeated and there was some change in the UN policy thereafter.

After that, I became the person to whom the UN staff at New York came. This was also due to the work of a Barbadian, 'Grasshat' Greaves who worked in the garage area. He touted my activities with more than a fair degree of Bajan pride. They all allowed me to park in an area which was off bounds to junior diplomats. Other members of staff from higher floors also came to me. I was therefore better informed than many of my colleagues. It was agreed then that I would become Chairman of the Fifth Committee the following year. The Ministry of Foreign Affairs in Bridgetown, however, had different ideas.

Ministers and Ministries always seemed to have

different ideas. I ran into a builder who was in the process of constructing a multi-storey (30 I believe) building on Second Avenue. He indicated that Barbados could purchase the building for $15 million. I passed on the message to a Minister I had worked for, but he simply said that there was no political constituency for such a purchase. The building could have housed all our offices in New York, provided a penthouse apartment for our Ambassador to the UN as well as a few staff members. The remaining floors could have been rented out and provided enough money to the Government of Barbados to run the entire Foreign Service.

I was to move on once again. Ambassador Oliver Jackman was in Washington. He was one of two great ambassadors I had the pleasure to work under. The other, much later, was Dr. Peter Laurie. The problem was that the officer being sent to Washington did not want to go there, so the new Ambassador to the UN was asked what he thought of having me go to Washington. When it was decided, a member of the UN School Board wrote, asking Foreign Affairs not to take away their representative from the School Board. The Permanent Secretary later asked me whom it was that I got to write the letter!

To add insult to injury, I was not granted monies for linen or a bookshelf, which were standard for other officers, and I had applied for a training course in New Zealand. I knew the Permanent Secretary would delay as long as possible, so I was ready to travel. He came back to indicate that I had been accepted the day before I was to travel. I was also due for home leave, so I made arrangements for my family to go on to Barbados. I left for the College in New Zealand for a six-week course in a little place outside Wellington. The course was divided into two sessions with a week between. I took the week off to have a look at the system of staff training and rotation New Zealand employed. They had a small Foreign Service, so there was likely to be something that we could learn from them. I wrote a report—I had had access to their highest officials—with some accompanying suggestions. The Permanent Secretary either destroyed the report or ensured in some way that it would not see the light of day.

It was only after I returned to New York, having spent two winters in one year, that I learnt that I had to leave for Washington once more. I could not believe that I had been so callously treated. But then, it had all happened before. All that I had achieved in New York was blighted by the way I continued to be treated by the folk in the Ministry. Fortunately, in the Washington Mission, I now had the cover of Ambassador Jackman, who understood to what use whatever skills I had, could be put.

Washington was familiar in all ways, except that my family was still in New York. Adé continued at Columbia and lived in Harlem. That brought with it some not so pleasant moments. A boy stole Tanya's bike while she was out on the street. Also on one weekend while I was visiting, someone broke into my car and stole the radio. There was a mass of wires hanging out from the dashboard. I was in doubt as to whether the car would start. It did. It was pointless reporting any of this to the police. Tanya however regained her bike. The boy was silly enough to ride past while her mother saw the bike. He was summarily removed from it. The radio probably went to buy some drug or other narcotic substance.

But Washington had one real advantage—Ambassador Jackman. He was always fair and never made a judgement before understanding the issue at hand in all its complexity. Twice I was attacked during that period; once when the Prime Minister visited Washington, and was to be taken back to the airport with the usual escort. The Foreign Minister was late for the start, so I drove in the cortege at over 70 miles an hour through Washington DC to accompany the Prime Minister. The Foreign Minister complained that there was no one to take him to the airport. That did not wash and nothing ever came of it. I also interviewed, along with Teresa Marshall, persons for the post of driver/messenger and we chose a Filipino, Nestor, who turned out not only to be a good and reliable driver, but on occasion acted as gardener at the Residence, repaired things that would otherwise have been thrown away, and he loved mauby. Indeed, he became something of an aficionado where mauby was concerned. He would make the drink from the tree bark. However, long before this, there was the complaint that Teresa Marshall, another officer, and I had chosen a Filipino instead of a Barbadian. Nestor, the new driver/messenger eventually became the Ambassador's driver.

My personal life changed considerably. My two

daughters came to live with me. Adé visited occasionally. We did not then intend to have another child, but in spite of the usual precautions, these occasional trysts resulted in a pregnancy. Adé finally returned to Washington, having completed all but her doctoral thesis and Wolé was born at Howard University hospital. He was so long that he had to be removed by Caesarean section. This was fortunate since the implant put in badly by a doctor to prevent the pregnancy would possibly have blinded or otherwise injured him.

For most of the time I spent in Washington, I lived in a beautiful house, which the Embassy had sensibly bought for the Deputy Head of Mission. It was large enough to house my mother when she decided to live in the Washington area after her course in nursing. It also made it possible to host the occasional friend, like Hugh Masakela or Ama Ata Aidoo or my cousin Pat Bannister. Memories of that house also included an incident when a Jamaican colleague of mine returned from Geneva and called my old telephone number. Some child had been calling my number and refusing to answer when I picked up the phone. I discovered this one day when I could hear the mother in the background saying that she had told her child not to call that number. So I had the telephone company change my number. My colleague, Cecile Clayton, called the old number to be told that I was not there. The number had already been re-assigned. She called a second time to be told more definitively that I was not there. Still believing that she had the correct number, she called a third time. This time the man at the other end said in a robotic voice: "This is a recording; Orlando does not live here." She then found me later at the office.

One other incident at the house occurred soon after I had had double glazed windows put in. There was a great snowstorm and the weight of the snow broke some of the electric lines. We were without heat. However, because of the insulation offered by the new windows, my family and I did not need to move to a hotel. We simply put on tracksuits and remained in the house for two nights and two days. The kids were delighted. It afforded them the excuse to all sleep in our bed. So there we were, five bodies in one king size bed. They were disappointed when the electricity was restored.

Interestingly, the Embassy as well as the second Residence had been fitted with the windows after I had been requesting funding for the operation for two years. I had finally found a contractor who said he could do the job using the most modern materials for half of what I had initially asked for. Typically my request had been cut in half, possibly with the notion that the retrofitting could be done in two stages. Oddly, after I had done the requisite scouting to find the contractor, the rumour in the Embassy was that I had received a cut back. Had I done so, it would have been something of a miracle, since the contract cost considerably less than any they had come up with.

What was amazing, however, was that the contractor came to Barbados with me, my family and Cardinal Warde, returning home for the first time in a long while. After he had done such honest and expert work at the Embassy and at the Counsellor's house, I asked him to make a back gate for the house we had bought in Wheaton. My mother, who was an excellent judge of character, opined that the contractor could milk a mouse running. I took no notice of her and gave him the $800 he said he needed for materials. I never saw him again.

My mother, who now lived with us, adored Wolé and treated him more like grandmothers do. Aderonké had once complained that Mom was too strict to be a grandmother, but Mom spared no effort in attempting to spoil Wolé. He would as soon as he could escape from his own bed, sneak across to Mom's bed. Adé or I would then recover him while he was asleep and return him to his room. He must have been most surprised in the morning.

One incident stands out during this period. I was sent to one of the several Barbadian celebrations in the mid-West. I met a young Jewish man who took me to his house. I was not allowed to shake his mother's hand because they were very strict orthodox Jews and only males of her household could touch her. What was most interesting was the story he told me about his own life. He was going out with a young woman who had three children from a man who was a drug trafficker. She was only twenty-three and had had to leave for the safety of her children. There had been lots of guns at the old house and a stash of two or three million dollars, a sort of float. When she left with the approval of her former man, he did not give her a large sum of money to keep the family going. She had to wait for an occasional disbursement for her and the children. It was the first time I had had a closer look at the US drug trade. Interestingly, he was only a minor trader in a small town.

But the most significant thing of that visit was that I met with the Barbadian tribe living there. Unlike their counterparts in Washington, they were very pleasant. I met them in a Prince Hall building, so I related the story of Prince Hall, a Bajan living in pre-independent America, who because racist attitudes did not allow him to join any US masonic lodge, applied to Britain for permission to start his own lodge and so the Prince Hall Lodge was born. Evidently, he was also possibly responsible for the creation of the Buffalo soldiers. George Washington is known to have granted him some arms, which would suggest that he was also part of the fight against the British,

Even before I had finished, an old gentleman in the crowd shouted: "Ah loves Yah!" That was typical of the mood of the audience. It received a giggle and then a cheer.

Most interesting of all was when Wolé was born. He was several weeks late, so I believed that I could get to Milwaukee and back before his birth, but he deceived me.

I had made one other interesting trip to meet with the local Barbadians. This was to Boston. There I met two of the local intellectuals as well as one of the St. Lucy Broomes, who was a very articulate pastor. But it was Professor Cardinal Warde who was the important new find. He was a Professor in Electrical Engineering at MIT. We chatted for a while and I suggested that he should return to Barbados at least on vacation, since he had not done so for many years. He accompanied me later to Barbados and his efforts here have been nothing short of spectacular. We maintained contact from then on, had dinner in Washington when he was there. When I was later Ambassador in Brussels, he called saying that he had a free afternoon and evening off after a conference in Amsterdam. I invited him down to Brussels. He arrived to have dinner not only with me, but also with the entire staff of the Embassy. It was a most enjoyable affair, and the staff members were delighted to have met such a distinguished Bajan.

Washington DC, The Second Round

IT WAS then too that I became familiar with Capitol Hill. I met several members of the Black Caucus who were to become very helpful later. I also got to learn who was who in the staff of the Ways and Means Committee. Ronald Reagan was now President and there was also a change of our Ambassadors. Our new man was not too familiar with the post. He once said on the telephone that he was British and on another occasion that he was pro-American. While there was nothing fundamentally wrong with being pro-American, he was not British and should definitely not have been broadcasting his international proclivities.

Initially, he was easy to work with. In fact, before he had been appointed, he and his wife who was my cousin had stayed with us in the Counsellor's Residence. However, when they broke up and divorced, he erroneously assumed that I would be in some way involved. So he would become suspicious of whatever I was doing. Before he had arrived, I had begun to lobby together with a lawyer hired by WIRSPA, the Caribbean rum group, for a removal of the high tariff on Caribbean rums. I had a good understanding with the President of WIRSPA, Patrick Mayers, who had indicated that supplies of rum as samples was not a problem and that he would be available to come to Washington at three days' notice. Very often, Congressmen liked to see an industry practicant rather than a Government representative.

He did not need to come very often, since the attorney, Doug Wachholtz, a blonde kinky haired Prussian American, and I roamed Capitol Hill talking mainly to Representatives of the House and winning new friends. We had put together a single page outlining the problem and our interest in having the $1.75 tariff on a wine gallon of rum removed. The tariff had been put there in the first place to protect Virgin Island and Puerto Rican rums. We made it clear that we were at the high end of the market and in no way likely to damage Puerto Rico or the Virgin Islands. Interestingly, it was the Virgin Islands Representative who objected to the removal of the tariff, even though they only supplied rums for mixes. Puerto Rico offered no real objection. It was therefore necessary to determine how we could paint the Virgin Islands in a less than positive light.

It happened that they were allowed to assemble watches in the US Virgin Islands and send them duty-free into the USA. Our supporters in the House of Representatives wanted to remove that privilege from the Virgin Islands. We had done less lobbying in the Senate, though we had some unlikely supporters there. We also had to do some work with sugar. We enlisted the assistance of an

American University Professor, Dr. Saud, whose students needed placements in businesses to complete their MBAs. Patrick Mayers agreed to have some of them at Goddard's Enterprises. I had also distributed some rum to members of the Ways and Means Committee, so there was always a seat somewhere in even the most packed meeting for me. A bill to remove the tariff from Caribbean rums was attached to a Ways and Means spending Bill. The House version also removed the duty-free privileges from the USVI. In Conference between the Senate and the House which had different bills on Caribbean rums—the Senate Bill only gave us limited tariff free entry—the Bill came out just as we wanted: free entry for Caribbean rums, but the retention of the Virgin Island privilege.

That process had taken all of two years of tramping up and down the Hill, but it was a serious success. After our huge success, one of the paid lobbyists on the Hill used to call me 'Mr. Rum', not because of any drinking capacity, but because against all odds I had managed to persuade Congress to add the Rum Bill to a Ways and Mean Bill which passed and gave Caribbean rums duty free entry into the USA. It also gave me access to first time Representatives like Beryl Anthony, who happened to be a friend of a later Governor of Arkansas and President of the USA, Bill Clinton. I remember once taking my new Ambassador to meet Representative Anthony. I walked in and the Congressman said: "Hello, Orlando." I quickly introduced my boss, hoping that he had not noticed that small hint of familiarity, which he never achieved at any such level, though Peter Laurie readily did.

It was also the moment when Reagan was planning the Caribbean Basin Initiative. This was largely to prop up the two countries he was supporting—Nicaragua and El Salvador—in their internecine wars. The rum deal was not part of the CBI. What was interesting here was that I managed to persuade a group from the House, led by the Speaker Tip O'Neill, to visit Barbados, at least to see another aspect of life in other Caribbean countries. I had cleared the offer with Trade Minister St. John and the Goddards agreed to take them on a boat tour.

Fascinatingly, when they returned, duly impressed with Barbados and their meetings there, occasionally one would hear from them something like "That was not our understanding of the situation when we were in Barbados." I was also then able to persuade Congressman Grey, the Chair of the Budget Committee, to set aside a small sum ($3million in scholarships) for the Eastern Caribbean States.

Early one Saturday morning after I had been up late on the Friday night before, I received a call from Prime Minister Adams. He had chosen to call me rather than the Ambassador. Half asleep, I heard something about Langley, the home of the CIA. I quickly asked him if he needed to be picked up from Langley. "No," he replied, "I said that I heard that you had moved and thought that you would have moved closer to Langley."

Fully awake now, I replied: "Oh no. I have in fact moved further into Maryland."

He then proceeded to tell me that he was not totally comfortable with what the US Ambassador told him about the CBI, so he wanted to check a few issues with me. He may have asked about ten questions in the next hour and I answered as fully and briefly as possible. He did not ask questions answerable in the negative or affirmative. I was amazed to read an interview he had had about an hour later at the airport. His answers were so full and detailed; one would have believed that he had been part of the entire CBI process.

President Reagan has retained a popularity that is rather more than deserved. He did a deal with Iran when they were holding US officials hostage. This included a deal not to release the hostages before he took office and the agreement to supply arms to that country, the money from which he used to purchase arms for the contras (whom he designated as the moral equivalents of the Founding Fathers) in Nicaragua. He was also an established racist, having spoken on the platform of Governor Wallace. Interestingly too, after winning the Republican Primary, he went to Philadelphia, a small town in Mississippi, not to his native California, to celebrate. There he made the infamous coded statement: "I believe in States' rights!" This was an outright commitment not to interfere in the segregationist policies of the South and thus win Mississippi.

He later mined the Managua harbour. My Ambassador thought that it was a left wing fiction that had spread this story! Even as a B-class actor, Reagan was able with his stories of the USA being a bright city on the hill and talk about a brighter day, to inspire a collectively paranoid Right Wing segment of the population (the rest of the world is out to get them), and have them believe that all was well under the Gipper.

The CBI achieved little. It was supposedly partly to improve the economies of the Region so that Communism (right wing Americans have a very different definition of Communism than most other people) could not spread throughout the Region. One obvious opportunity for Reagan came in the form of a left wing Government in Grenada. After the US use of snipers to eradicate operatives they did not like in Beirut, radicals in Lebanon retaliated by destroying the US Embassy there. This was a shocking defeat. Reagan needed an easy victory. So with the help of some Caribbean Governments, he invaded Grenada ostensibly to save the US students there from attack by left wing forces. The first achievement of that attack was the destruction of the mental hospital in St. George. The students were moved to safety, not by the attacking forces, but before the US soldiers could reach them!

Just before this posting, I had had the opportunity to be in Barbados for a while, together with my wife and children. I now had a one-year-old son, Wolé. I was able to introduce him to my father, who had been ill for quite a while. It had been diagnosed as muscular dystrophy, but that condition usually leads to a relatively quick death. It was more likely to have been Lou Gehrig's disease. However, when my father was first afflicted, what happened was that he became gradually weaker in his limbs. We used to take him to the beach. He had always loved the sea. It was sad seeing this man, who could swim the breadth of Carlisle Bay, now crippled. It became even worse and he had to remain in bed all the time.

He was in this condition when we visited. My second daughter, Ronké, spent the entire visit with Dads as my eight siblings called him. She massaged his limbs and spoke to him. When he eventually died I returned to Barbados for the funeral. Ronké was later furious that I had not taken her. I had believed that it would have been traumatic for her. She objected to the fact that the decision had been made without consulting her. She was eight years old.

Dads had been a fine man. He had a few friends, including his neighbour in Eagle Hall, TP and Mr. Armstrong and the old farmer, Mr. Phillips. He was probably the most diligent worker I have ever known. His wife Hilda never worked outside the house and the children came too fast for him ever to 'catch himself' as he would have put it. He therefore had to work all the time to be able to put food on the table. In fact he even worked during his vacation so that he could buy clothes for the children. He was also generous to a fault. He seldom thought about himself. Indeed, when I had won a Barbados Scholarship, he congratulated me and suggested that I should go out there, make my mother proud and take care of her. It hurt when he died, but knowing how much he would have suffered quietly, I was not unhappy that his life had ended.

Caracas

I WAS now transferred to Caracas. The new Minister of Foreign Affairs informed me simply that he could find no one else who spoke Spanish! I had just arrived when I, as Chargé d'Affaires, was called into the Venezuelan Ministry of Foreign. I was prepared for a thrashing on the matter of the invasion of Grenada, as I was sure that the Venezuelan military would have taken a dim view of the USA invading a Caribbean country. Indeed they did, but the Ministry was of a different view. They informed me that they supported the Barbados position, but had to call me in because it was necessary to give the correct impression to the less compliant military.

I learned later from Prime Minister Adams that when Coard and his military people had imprisoned Maurice Bishop, the populist former leader of Grenada, the UK, Barbados and Venezuela had cooked up a plan to free Bishop, take him out of Grenada and thus ease the tension that had built up in that country. The UK would have provided a ship out to sea, while the Venezuelans with a speed motorboat would smuggle a Barbados team into St. George to release Bishop and take him back to the mother ship. Regrettably, this plan had been calculated to take place the night of the same day that a crowd had broken down the door of the detention house and let Bishop out only to have him murdered by the military. Prime Minister Adams, who had tacitly supported the US invasion, made an effort to prevent the Grenadian Foreign Minister from returning to the chaos there. Mr. Louison had, however, said that he had to return. He was one of those slaughtered along with Maurice Bishop.

My sojourn in Caracas was relatively brief—eight months. It was a hard post since my family remained in the Washington area, as the international school in Caracas was not recommended, and the Permanent Secretary who had been removed as our last Ambassador to Venezuela ensured that the Chargés d'Affaires who succeeded him would not be granted the Ambassadorial allowances they were rightfully entitled to. I therefore had to live on the edge, since my base salary had to go towards sustaining my family, now four in number, to pay their rent, food etc. The stint did, however, improve my Spanish, which was negligible when I arrived in Caracas. I could correct the colloquialisms of the bi-lingual secretary, whose two languages really were Bajan and Caraceno, a Caracas dialect. And I could conduct a conversation in bad Costeno, the Spanish dialect of the Caribbean area, Chile and the Canary Islands.

It was in one respect New York all over again. It was the same Permanent Secretary with the same modus operandi. I recommended that we place the monies on the number One account (monies collected by the

Embassy, which could only be spent on the permission of Parliament) into an account, which offered 13% interest. I was informed that I had not been sent there to make money for the Government. So the money remained on an account which did not accrue any interest at all!

I was also slated to attend a meeting in Lima, Peru. Typically, permission only came at the eleventh hour. I called the bank, which was officially closed, but they promised to let my driver in. I called the Peruvian Embassy, since I needed a visa, and they agreed to keep the Embassy open for another half an hour. I sent the driver with a note to the bank, and since I did not know Caracas particularly well, I took a secretary with me to the Peruvian Embassy. So I was off to Lima, which was interesting and accommodating until my last few minutes there. The meeting had gone well. I would have hoped that I could visit Cusco or Machu Picchu, but since I had not requested any leave I had to console myself with a visit to the incredible ruins in Lima itself. These were testimony to the existence of an Inca-like period of three different settlements with things like sewing rooms for women etc. One unpleasant incident occurred when I had already cleared immigration and was waiting for the plane to arrive. An official of some sort came up to me and asked to see my passport. I replied in loud Spanish that the only reason he had chosen me to ask for a passport was because I was black. He was duly embarrassed and desisted.

Prime Minister Adams came to Caracas on a state visit while I was there. His "You were the only one I could find who can speak Spanish" Foreign Minister, refused to stand in for the Prime Minister when the latter became ill. He had accompanied the Prime Minister on the visit. I was forced to stand in for the Prime Minister and seemed to have managed reasonably well.

Prime Minister Adams was later into his usual game-playing mode. He told me he was trying to work out some tangent that would help him calculate the distance between Caracas and Bridgetown. He was a brilliant mathematician and a very sharp intellect. I said that, according to my calculation, the figure was about 11. He replied that he thought it was more like 11.8. I responded that I did not have a slide rule: hence my inaccuracy. He seemed to like the fact that someone could have that sort of conversation with him. It later occurred to me that the two best Prime Ministers Barbados had had been Errol Barrow and Tom Adams. It was said that Adams openly admired Barrow and Barrow admired Tom in secret.

I was shipped back to Washington. Prime Minister Adams with whom I had had considerable contact as a result of the Grenada affair, wanted to appoint me Ambassador to Venezuela, but the Permanent Secretary concocted some story about me. I later learnt from my file that the Permanent Secretary had removed the note he had sent to the Prime Minister. The note must have said that I did not write particularly well etc. etc. The Prime Minister replied that I wrote particularly well and that he trusted my advice more than the Permanent Secretary's. It was then that the PS concocted yet another story about me and told the PM personally. Mr. Adams sent me back to Washington.

He visited the USA for the last time before he died. On this occasion, Steve Emtage, then the economic guru of the Barbados Government, came along. We had the discomfort of riding in the car that was armed to protect the PM. The blonde gunman looked like a Hollywood stereotype, and each time he shifted his weapon to train it on someone in traffic that he thought suspicious, we shuddered.

What was interesting about that visit was the Prime Minister's nimbleness of foot, so to speak. Steve Emtage sat on one side of him and I on the other during a session with journalists. Every time the journalists asked him a question about trade issues, Steve would come up with figures on a slip of paper. The hot topic then was about the USA offering arms to Caribbean countries. At one point, I slipped him a note warning him that the military question was coming. We merely slipped him bits of paper and without missing a beat he would glance down at the paper and respond. When the question of arms for Barbados came, he responded that he would be happier if the offer was for some form of beeper so that when our fishermen got lost out to sea, they could alert nearby shipping. GPS had not yet been invented. The journalists however got the message: Barbados was not interested in arms.

Working with Prime Minister Errol Barrow was also a delight. The first time I did was during the fuel crisis of the early 70s. I rode a bicycle to work in Foreign Affairs, had a shower there and changed into my work clothes. It was at a meeting of Heads of the newly formed CARICOM. Prime Minister Manley said it was rather late for me to be up. I replied loud enough for Prime Minister Barrow to hear that this was the duty of a civil servant. He mumbled something about my not knowing what I was talking about.

That was not the first time that we had disagreed about one thing or another. On one occasion when cricket was on at Kensington—and we played cricket then—he saw me going back into work and asked how come I was not at cricket. I simply informed him that not everyone could go to cricket on the same day if there was work to be done. He again dismissed this explanation.

However, every other meeting with him was less combative and he was extremely funny. When we arrived in Kingston for a Commonwealth Heads of Government Meeting, his dear friend, Prime Minister Michael Manley, had sent him a long Cadillac as his personal car. He told the driver that he should inform his PM that we had enough hearses in Barbados and that he would like a normal car.

He had reserved a large slot of time for briefing before the meeting began. A French Canadian media company, wanting to do an interview in French, had already contacted him. When the Prime Minister of Grenada, Eric Gairy heard that our PM was doing an interview and he was not, he tore into his assistants only to learn that the interview was to be conducted in French, a language he did not speak.

Steve Emtage briefed the PM on the economic matters before he got to the question of the interview. He pointed out that his slant would be that we are all interdependent and he wanted to throw in a quote from his favourite Jacobean poet, John Dunne: "No man is an island unto himself." He wanted that rendered in French. Oliver Jackman and I both responded simultaneously that the line was not easily rendered in French. "Well," Mr. Barrow continued, "Then I will say it in English and they will know that I am bilingue (bilingual in French)!"

He did have an excellent command of the French language. On a much later occasion when he had a meeting with General Namphy in an effort to persuade the General to hold elections in Haiti, he told the interpreter to stop the interpretation. Peter Laurie and I were part of that delegation. I was a bit amazed, because Namphy spoke a creolised French that was not that easy to understand. However, discussing the issues with the Prime Minister later, it was clear that he had understood everything that Namphy had said. I later learnt that Prime Minster Barrow had grown up in the Virgin Islands and had not spoken English for a long time. His mother, who wondered why, happened to wander into the kitchen one day and hear him conversing with a boxer cum singer (Canada Lee, a sort of forerunner of Paul Robeson) in Danish, the former language of those islands.

The last occasion on which I had the pleasure of

working with him was when he was on his way to Atlanta for a Human Rights Meeting. Peter Laurie, who was then my Ambassador, despatched me to Miami to meet Prime Minister Barrow. We had deliberately scheduled his flight to arrive in Miami on a Saturday so that he could have some rest. Colin Mayers, then Honorary Consul, now Consul-General in Miami, was there with me when he arrived. He insisted on going directly to the hotel. He hated to have security around him all the time. He wanted to do some minor shopping, but that could wait until Sunday. So we talked about all sorts of issues. He also reminisced about his wartime days. What stands out from that account was one of his forty flights over Germany.

He was returning to Canada and he was the pilot. They saw two strings of light below and the captain wanted to land. Mr. Barrow insisted that they should not land. They had not yet reached Nova Scotia, and in any case, there were airports all the way to Vancouver. Naturally, there was a blackout and lights only appeared when a Canadian flight was about to land. The captain took his advice and they continued and actually landed in Nova Scotia. The following day, he noticed that one of his friends was missing. He assumed the worst, only to be delighted to see him a few days later. "What happened?" he asked.

"Man," his friend replied, "We damn nearly got drowned. We saw these two rows of lights and came down only to land out in the ocean between two lines of shrimp boats!"

We continued the session until just after midnight.

Mr. Barrow said we would meet again the following day, but not too early. The following day, he called me just before 6.00 am to indicate that Colin Mayers was on his way, so could I come down. I arrived before Colin. He indicated that he had already spoken to his Ministers about various issues. He then asked me whether I wanted next to be posted (as Ambassador) to Caracas. President Jaime Lusinchi of Venezuela was his personal friend. I replied that I would be more comfortable with Brussels. In diplomacy, an officer should strenuously avoid being placed between two ruling friends. "Well," he continued, "Brussels it will be. I will inform Cammie Tudor (the Foreign Minister). He will be alright with it."

Colin turned up and we went shopping at a pharmacy. The security was incredible. All normal shoppers had to get out of the way while my Prime Minister combed the shelves for whatever things he wanted to buy. Mr. Barrow shopped as quickly as he could and returned to the hotel.

By now, my marriage was falling apart. I had been separated from my wife for long periods of time. She had completed all but her thesis at Columbia, but showed no interest in researching or writing her doctoral thesis. Indeed, throughout this whole period, except for one year when she taught at Howard University, she did not work at all, since we had had the services of a housekeeper cum nanny for all the years before I was transferred to

Venezuela. We had had a delightful little son, who was very bright, but also seemed inevitably to get into fights at school. I always had to rescue him. At home, if he threw a tantrum, his elder sister Tanya managed him beautifully. She would take him aside and talk to him and return with a perfectly peaceful child.

Wolé, my son, was the only one of the three who showed no particular interest in singing. I had been a second tenor in the Barbados Festival choir—not a star role, but it did mean that I could sing. I had also sung in smoke-filled clubs in Stockholm and chain-smoked when I first arrived in Sierra Leone. My two daughters sang well. Tanya, the elder daughter, often sang at meal times. One day when she had reached the final high notes of *Tomorrow* from Annie, Wolé accompanied her and hit every note perfectly. He then proceeded to applaud. He was perhaps two at the time.

During the period where my wife worked, we sold a parcel of land that we owned in Barbados, and bought a house in Maryland. The children were all in school in Maryland. The question was now whether we should split up as a family with my wife and two daughters remaining in Maryland and our son coming with me. That was not acceptable to my wife who wanted to leave Tanya at school in the area, come with the other two and fly back to Columbia University maybe twice a year to complete her thesis. She did not, at any account, wish me to take Wolé with me to Brussels. I wanted a divorce. She insisted that she did not want one, even though later she filed for a divorce.

I suggested that we do it amicably, that I would continue to pay the mortgage on the Maryland property, pay the children's school fees and provide an element of support for them all. She felt there was more to be had and we ultimately paid enormous lawyers' fees; she retained the house in Maryland and I the one in Barbados, a poor equivalency. It was clear that the judge did not like me. He even suggested that after Brussels, I would return to some fancy job in the USA. I rather boldly informed him that I was unaware that there were fancy jobs waiting for anyone looking like me. He did not dare defend racism, so he let the comment ride.

A few months after our disagreement, I was recalled from Washington to Barbados in preparation for Brussels. While I was back home, I ran into Prime Minister Barrow once. He was at the Government Information Service in Bay Street. He had at that time written two cook books and I asked him when he would write something about his political life. I also asked about his languages. To the former he said that he would write it all down soon and that his best foreign language was actually Italian. He died a few weeks later. I heard the news at a bridge tournament where I was playing. I was stunned.

Later after the public had demanded a public ceremony (the great man had wanted to have a quiet incineration and minor ceremony), it was granted. People had called in to say that it was their Prime Minister and now that he had passed on they had the right to decide how he should be celebrated. It fell to the lot of Messrs Laurie and Johnson and myself to arrange the meeting of all the foreign delegates, providing them with vehicles and accommodation for the occasion. In spite of the sheer bedlam of late flights, persons arriving unexpectedly inter alia, we had it all well arranged until the police decided that they would take care of the parking of vehicles at the stadium. We wanted to have the VIP cars parked on the outside of the other cars. The police mixed it all up and the VIP cars were situated anywhere in the mix. The great man, the late Errol Barrow, was later named one of our national heroes.

Brussels

One day while I was in the Ministry, a journalist called asking if it was correct that X, Y and Z were being posted to different missions including Brussels. I was nowhere in the mix and I indicated that I could not comment. He had got all his information from some totally unreliable source. Not one of the postings he had heard of was correct. For the first time I was struck by the fact that I would not be working with Prime Minister Barrow.

Almost as soon as I reached Brussels, an offer came to the Embassy, which I was sure Mr. Barrow would have at least investigated. A well-established ship wreck operation's head wanted to set up in Barbados to search for sunken wealth between Barbados and West Africa. His operation was to be centred in Barbados; he would hire some Barbadians as crew members both for his ships as well as the mother ship and he would pay whatever taxes were relevant in Barbados.

It took the relevant Ministry some six weeks to reply and then they came up with the ridiculous question as to whether the operation would not infringe on Barbados' sovereignty. When I responded that it would even be possible to monitor what Japanese and Korean boats were fishing with their long lines in Barbados' territorial waters, it still took another two months. The businessman became sick of the delay and sited his operation in Costa Rica.

A second early failure had to do with sea-island cotton. I had trumpeted the virtue of this product only grown in a handful of Caribbean islands and an Italian group wanted to absorb all the cotton we could produce in the Region, make the lint in Barbados and later have an Italian couturier make the finished products in Barbados. When I returned to Barbados to see if this was agreeable, I was informed that we had already signed a contract with the Japanese to sell them all our cotton. That later turned out to be an error.

Then there was the matter of bagasse. Two Italians who visited with me wanted to convert bagasse into animal feed. They were prepared to set up the conversion plant in Barbados. This time I went directly to Erie Deane, who was the head of the Sugar Producers' Association. We were producing nearly 100 tonnes of sugar at that time, which meant that we had at least 900 tonnes of bagasse. I was simply told that Barbados had no bagasse. Bagasse was then either burnt in the factory or thrown onto cane fields. It is only now that we have made any effort—thanks to David Estwick, a Minister who thinks ahead—that we have diversified and realise the wide range of products that can be had from the sugar cane.

I had asked Oliver Jackman what Brussels was like. In typical fashion, he replied: "It is a beautiful, grey city." I have never heard a better brief description of that city. So I was off to Brussels and settled into the beautiful Residence that Barbados owns there. The place had been bought during the tenure of Oliver himself. He had identified the house when a Minister happened to be in Brussels. They both agreed on its suitability and price and in atypical public service fashion, the sale was completed in short order. It is still the most beautiful of the Residences we own. It is situated obliquely opposite a chateau owned by Mobotu.

The chateau occupied a block in the prestigious neighbourhood. It had two guard towers at the front and extensive gardens behind the castle. The gardens had a miniature bridge, running over a small ditch, and were impeccably manicured. My teenage daughter Tanya came back into the Residence one day and said that she, Ronké and Wolé had tried to get into the park, but the gate was closed. She had assumed that the gardens of the Mobotu palace were a public park.

The Barbados Residence had a beautiful tennis court, which I was able to use very effectively in promoting my access to DGVIII, the segment of the European Commission responsible for relations with the African, Caribbean and Pacific (ACP) group of countries. It had two flowering plants in front of the house and a swimming pool at the rear of the house. It was fit for any Representative of any country.

Oliver Jackman had also indirectly offered some advice. He indicated that when one was an Ambassador, the way people behaved toward you sometimes made you feel larger than life. The advice did not much bother me, since I knew that I would always be me. However, when I arrived in Brussels a staff member suggested that I should not be too 'familiar' with everyone since that would lose me respect. I took no notice of that either because being different would have prevented me from being me. So I kept up my jovial nature and spoke with anyone without fear or favour. It was simply my intention always to be me.

For the first time in my career, I did not have to concern myself about having my personal effects moved. I had at one point moved six times in a seven-year period! I settled in quickly, and after about 35 days wrote the Permanent Secretary my assessment of the issues we faced. I separated the issues into different pages so that they could easily go on to the different files in the Ministry of Foreign Affairs. The PS replied that if I wrote so much after one month, he could not calculate how much I would write in a year!

One of my first acts in Brussels was to request of the Tourist Board that they send a musical team of Gabby, Grynner and Square One to a festival they held in Hoogstraaten each year. Hoogstraaten is a small Belgian town near the Dutch border. I went to the festival there where they had some sort of Caribbean music. I approached the organiser and suggested that I could provide him with the best performers in the business.

I must have been sufficiently persuasive, since he agreed

to pay for the accommodation and local transport of the group while they were in Belgium. My next task was to persuade the Tourist Board to arrange for them to get to Belgium and back and to provide some element of per diem. There was also the possibility of an airline picking up the travel. I was going home that year, so I could try to iron out any possible difficulties. There were difficulties. The Tourist Board person hummed and hawed and I finally said that I was returning to Brussels and she could do whatever she wanted.

Almost at the last moment, the group was provided with some money and they arrived in Brussels. At the first concert, which was held in Hoogstraaten, Alison Hinds wore a tight-fitting outfit, did her dance and belted out some beautiful music. There was a man up front who stood there with his mouth wide open. If he had managed to breathe in, he would probably have swallowed her. Gabby and Grynner received equally great adoration. Afterwards, I invited them all to the Residence for a meal. Interestingly, Grynner was the only one who drank; there were a couple of vegetarians, including Gabby and no one smoked.

Their next stop was in another small town, Lokeren, known for its football. There was a not very good rock group on the stage and there was a scattering of young people in attendance in the square. When Square One came on to the stage, it began to rain. In spite of that, the square filled up and when the group sang *Take Something and Wave*, the young men took off their T-shirts and waved the wet garments vigorously.

The group was invited then to perform in Germany for a TV show, where Gabby became an instant star. I was nonetheless questioned as to whether Germany had been part of the original tour plan. I simply replied that it cost nothing more for the Board and Germany was indeed part of my gebeit.

I became even bolder and arranged for them to perform in Stockholm in front of the Opera Square. I took some time off and accompanied them. Stockholm was not part of the area for which I had any diplomatic responsibility, but I had studied, taught and lived there. I had friends there, so there was no difficulty for me when once I had arranged my leave. There was quite an interesting gathering in the Square. We were supposed to finish by 11.00 pm, but the police extended this by half an hour. Gabby had a sore throat, so Alison picked up the slack by doing a Bob Marley medley, which sent the crowd wild. Someone had said to me after his calypsonian had finished just before the Bajan group began that no one could better his man's performance. He was totally wrong. Even after our group was finished singing, the crowd did a Congo line and continued to sing: "Hot, Hot, Hot." Gabby got a contract to sing in Finland later that year and Square One became ready for an international career.

Back at the Embassy, there was the question of my secretary. She had not yet been appointed even though every Embassy was supposed to have a Secretary to the Ambassador. Additionally, she had been acting for twelve years, partly under my predecessors and at the Tourist Board in London. I wrote a strong letter on her behalf and she was appointed and the twelve years counted as part of her service. She later went on to do a degree at the University of Maryland in Brussels. That too required a bit of assistance, since, attending some classes, she needed half a day. I suggested that two half days constituted a whole day and that she could spend as much of her vacation allowance as was necessary. The only excluded time was during Council Meetings where all hands were needed. She obtained her degree there and was later promoted to Deputy Head of Mission in Miami! No wonder she, Gaile Thompson, was one of the two best secretaries I have ever had.

The Permanent Secretary was later to arrange a transfer to the Mission of someone who I thought he believed would be disruptive and so have us both discredited. This was Carl Jackson, who had made himself rather unpopular by being sent to Grenada over the wishes of the then Permanent Secretary by Prime Minister Adams and then, on top of it, doing an excellent job there. Carl had subsequently returned to Barbados and not been promoted. He came to Brussels rather disgruntled.

It took a while for him to settle in. Then, on one occasion he made a serious error of conduct. I called him aside and told him why I thought he had been sent to Brussels, and that we were in fact in a situation where he had to look out for my back and I his. He took the message to heart and performed well thereafter. He was soon promoted to Counsellor. He was a brilliant writer and could encapsulate ideas in a form that was sometimes spectacular. He was the only 'junior' officer, beside Anne-Marie Blackman, whom I felt had the sort of abilities of Oliver Jackman or Peter Laurie. Peter Laurie had once responded to a complaint from the State Department that we voted against the US position more often than we voted with them. This had been typical of the complaint sent in annually. Peter replied that since more than half of UN votes were by consensus, this could not be correct. Additionally, the issues on which we disagreed, such as South Africa and the Palestinian question, represented more of a disagreement between friends. We could follow the USA blindly, but that would be more of a relationship between master and servant than between friends. The State Department never again sent us that annoying note, at least not during the time we were at the Embassy. Jackson could capture that tone.

I remember him on one occasion helping me frame a letter to the Belgian Ministry of Foreign Affairs in rejoinder to a letter they sent to the Embassy. Europe produced the better-known racists like Hegel, Gobineau, Chamberlain, Wagner, and Hitler et al. This also left a seemingly undying effect on many ordinary Europeans, among whom Belgians tend to seem to want to be counted. Thus one day, when a junior officer came back to the Embassy and the two official cars were parked in the two allocated spaces on the street in front of the Embassy, he quickly got out and asked the Embassy driver to move one car forward so that he could park on the small lawn area. Before he could complete the manoeuvre, two policemen came up and said he could not park out on the street. He was obviously not parking, so he proceeded to reverse into the lawn area. (The police on one occasion arrested and beat the Counsellor of an African Embassy while he was trying to enter the Embassy Building! That Ambassador lodged no complaint. I would certainly not have acquiesced in any such horror).

I ignored the incident until a note came from the Foreign Ministry with the police report appended in Dutch, complaining about our behaviour. I could read enough Dutch already at that time to understand the police report. It began by saying that as they were driving along the street, they noticed a "man of colour" had stopped. They got out and went to him and he almost ran them over. Interestingly, my officer had reversed and the two police officers were in front of the car. We wrote back explaining that we were unaware that it was an offence to be a man of colour since that was what was immediately noticed and that it would have been impossible to run over two policemen in front of a car when that car was reversing. We added that we were saddened that two such officers could sully the reputation of what was otherwise a fine police force. That diplomatic lie ensured that we never again heard from the Ministry on any such issue for the remainder of my long sojourn in Belgium.

I should point out that this was the only occasion I came face to face with Belgian racist behaviour. The reality was that as Ambassador, I was generally sheltered. I do, on the other hand, remember an act of extreme friendliness. I happened to be in a plush supermarket and a Belgian lady pointed out to me that her son wanted to kiss me. I had no idea what that was all about, but when I picked the youngster up, he kissed me on the cheek.

It was suggested to me that my friendliness with juniors and ordinary members of the ACP Secretariat would lose me respect. Indeed, one African colleague once complained to a member of the European Commission that I laughed too much. He failed to understand that funny people are often the most serious. The Commission official reminded him of this in a terse reply. "That may be," he said, "But when Ambassador Marville says anything, I take it very seriously." To the credit of my colleagues in general, I developed great friendships particularly with Ambassadors Iroha and Katungi of Nigeria and Uganda respectively, the Ambassador of Dominica who ultimately became President of that country, and Madame de St. Jorre, who became the Foreign Minister of the Seychelles. One other Ambassador noted that when I spoke of Barbados, it was evident how much I loved my country. That was the greatest compliment of them all.

Josh Iroha, on one occasion, was in a meeting of the African Group when a Francophone Ambassador complained about the Caribbean Group. Josh got up and informed the meeting that they were talking about his people and he would have none of that. Nigeria was enough of a force in the Group for him to make this comment.

Josh Iroha and Charles Katungi often played tennis at the Residence. I remember one fabled day when the three of us played what we called Australian doubles. No one could reach a winning total at the end of several rounds. Charles was eager to continue even though it was practically nightfall and thus dark. Josh simply said: "Man, it is dark and I cannot see, so we are finished."

Josh had gone to public school in the UK and knew personally people like Tony Benn, with whom he had shared a place at a British public school; he had functioned as an executive in BASF in Germany, and was a superb financial expert. Charles had worked in Nairobi with UNEP and was an extremely good-looking, always well-dressed and charming man. On one occasion, Charles overheard the then head of DGVIII in the Commission say that he played tennis every day at lunch. We also knew that his deputy Philippe Soubestre was a very fine tennis player, so we invited the two of them to play at the Barbados Residence one Saturday afternoon. We were fortunate to have had excellent weather that day. Frankly, they were together better than Charles and myself, but Charles and I played way above our heads and beat them on that day. Thereafter, we played and they won more than they lost. But that first day was special.

The tennis court is just outside the kitchen window, so in the absence of any staff, it was easy to ferry water, beer and tea out very easily between sets. We must have between the four of us drunk eight mugs of tea, two or three gallons of water and about ten or more beers. The ritual pouring of liquid from our bodies established a very real friendship. The older official, who had been relatively cold before, was approachable on the issue of rum and he told me that the obstacle I had to deal with was a former German Professor in the Commission. So I engaged the German.

Wes Hall, who was then Minister of Tourism, came on a visit dealing with tourism. He found out what the EU wanted as distinct from what was in Barbados' interest and 'buried' the German.

As usual, the EU wanted to pack any technical assistance programme with its own consultants. Minister Hall simply said that he was prepared to return to his Cabinet Colleagues and inform them that some little person in the Commission had been unprepared to listen to his reasonable demands. The German official immediately reversed his position and agreed to a compromise position. I whispered to the Minister that he should now thank him. The Minister quoted Mark Anthony's speech over Julius Caesar's slain body in the Shakespeare play. "I come to bury Caesar, not to praise him."

The official asked whether he was now to be buried? The Minister replied quite bluntly: "I have already buried you, I now wish to praise you." Not all that long after—although I doubt that there was any connection—that official disappeared from the scene and I had a younger and more flexible German to deal with. Philippe Soubestre also became the boss of the Division at that time. His old boss had retired and the position stayed with France.

Philippe was perhaps the most hard-working individual in the Commission. He read every document and knew every detail. It was therefore easy to discuss any issue with him. He in turn was fair, while never revealing the position of the EU on any matter that was under consideration. He often stayed on in his office until the wee hours of the morning. (I usually spoke to his wife in French even though she worked in English, while I spoke English to Philippe, since he was from the Bordeaux region of France and spoke accordingly.) She understood his late hours. He was also like Charles Katungi, a great dresser. In fact, at one meeting where Charles wore this magnificent suit, Philippe turned up in exactly the same suit, with similar tie and a slightly different shirt. I never saw either one of them wear that suit again. To make matters worse, the Commission's chairman of the meeting said that he noticed that there was such a level of agreement between the two sides that they were even wearing the same uniform! I thought only females reacted like this. I was most surprised that it could happen to two such macho males.

Also interesting about this occasion where Charles was the ACP speaker and Philippe, the Commission's was Charles' opening remarks. He had written his speech in English, but realising that French, which he did not speak, had similar sounds to his native Kinyawanda, asked me to read a French translation of his speech to him. He transcribed the sounds he heard into Kinyawanda. He then read the sounds he had written down to the ACP-EU audience. It came out in perfectly intelligible French. Everyone was amazed. When it was Philippe's turn to speak, he began by saying (even though he could have) that he was not going to imitate his colleague and speak in English!

Although I was accredited to the BENELUX countries, Italy, Germany and Austria (where Waldheim was President), I spent most of my time working on issues related to the ACP-EU partnership. It was physically impossible to spend more time on non-ACP issues. I was specifically interested in issues of trade, especially rum. When they elected me Chairman of the Trade Committee, I had to look after not only rum, but also bananas, rice and sugar as well as items like yams and sweet potatoes, which Barbados also exported to the UK. The Europeans were stubborn even when they were wrong. They wanted, for instance, to impose a quota on sweet potatoes and yams, which they claimed were animal food! Even when they were duly corrected, they still imposed a quota, which was of course somewhat more ample.

I did, however, achieve a significant breakthrough in rum. We had constant battles with the Dutch (like the Germans) making rumverschnitt, a mixture of heavy rum with potato alcohol, the Danes making a liqueur called rum and the Greeks making some liquor and calling it Caribbean rum. With the help of the French who wanted to preserve their rum industry in the departements, we also secured a definition of rum, which ultimately preserved the industry. Germany was allowed to continue making rumverschnitt, but Holland was not. The Greeks had to desist from their fraud.

There were several issues that remained. In this whole process, Cockspur was most helpful. Their CEO supplied me with whatever quantity of old rum I needed, just as he had done in Washington. I ensured that the Commissioner for DGVIII had a continuous supply. (On one occasion he ran out and said loudly at the end of an ACP-EU meeting, "Orlando, I have no more rum.") I also supplied the gentleman who dealt with rum and several of my friends. I even arranged once with the Ambassador of Togo at a meeting in Lomé, Togo, that we would have only Togolese beer, Ugandan gin (made from bananas) and Bajan rum. We pulled it off and the Europeans got terribly besotted. I naturally, later, exchanged old rum for two bottles of vintage KVV port with my South African colleague.

There were two final hurdles with rum. DGVIII assumed that heavy rums were only made for sale to the Germans for making verschnitt. It took me sometime to discover that they did not understand that spiced Trinidadian rums also fell into that category, so the quota fell off. The final thrust was to change the segmented way rum was allowed into the EU. Initially Caribbean rums could only be imported on a progressive basis to countries, which normally imported our rums. The percentage was negligible, so if one had exported 10 cases to Italy, it made little sense going after the Italian market. Only the UK and Germany were serious markets. Eventually, the entry of rum was de-segmented and the rum industry could move from perhaps somewhere in the mid-sixty per cent factory usage to over 90 per cent.

I did occasionally get out of the normal run of trade and other obvious diplomatic duties. I went, as I indicated, on my first year to a festival held in Hoogstraaten and other Belgian towns during the summer. There was the musical affair in Hoogstraaten.

Efforts at creating opportunities in Barbados itself were less successful. I had developed a great rapport with the Italian Trade representative in Brussels.

During my sojourn in Brussels, there was little in the way of family life. In my first summer there, my mother, Aunt Gwen, her sister, my three children and young Jasmine, Aunt Gwen's granddaughter came to visit. My mother wanted to go to Sweden, since I had been there. She always wanted to visit places I had been to. We took off in one car. The two small ones, Jasmine and my son Wolé were bored so they started a chorus: "Look, a cow!"

Our first stop was in Germany for lunch. Ronké waited until we had eaten most of the ordered meal and asked if we had finished. She proceeded to demolish what remained. The following night, it was Wolé's turn. It was a spaghetti dinner. This was in Denmark where we had to sleep over. We completed the journey on the following day.

In Sweden, we stayed at the house of my old friend from university days, Ahmadu Jah. Mom cooked and Ahmadu's young son and daughter stayed with us and ate. Ahmadu's ex, who had stayed in my house in Barbados, was annoyed that we were there, since she and Ahmadu now had a dispute about the house. She was quite wealthy and now lived with a man who also had a house, but she wanted to have this house as well. Ahmadu had suggested that she could take the apartment, which he also owned, and let the children have the house. She insisted and he gave in. Nonetheless, our stay was otherwise very pleasant. We also visited my old friend from Stockholm University days and later in Ghana and Cameroon, Birgitta Abrahamsson. Her 'sambo' (common law husband) Ulf entertained the children royally. Wolé evidently reminded him of the son of an old Ugandan colleague and he toted Wolé around on his shoulder and Jasmine tagged along.

The following summer, my three children visited, and we decided to go to Crete, Greece. We went with a Belgian friend, Nicholas de Kerchove and his girlfriend and stayed in Nicholas' Cretan compound somewhere in the countryside. It was like an African compound, with one entrance in a circular yard with different cottages forming the perimeter of the compound. We also travelled to the famous Samaria Gorge, located beyond the mountains, by boat. Libya lies on the opposite side of the sea and is in fact closer than the Greek mainland.

Arrived there, I suffered an attack of vertigo, but believed that it was seasickness. I was never a good sailor. So I opted to walk the 16 kms through the gorge rather than return by boat. Nicholas agreed to walk with me and Tanya said she would have to accompany the two old men! The girlfriend and the two smaller children returned by boat and agreed to meet us at the top of the mountain, where the gorge began, in six hours.

The first 10 kilometres were not that difficult. We drank water from fountains that were scattered along the way. Tanya, who had to go to the bathroom almost every time she drank anything, was so dehydrated that she always eagerly awaited the next fountain, usually two kilometres away. We also ate a small lunch at a restaurant somewhere before the 10 km mark. The last 6 kilometres were two kilometres uphill. I pumped my fist on reaching the top in the manner of sportsmen everywhere these days. That was tougher, but we finished in just under the six hours we had calculated. The mountaintop was cold in the shade, so we sat outside a small café in the sun. It was now late afternoon. We must have consumed between the three of us: four cups of tea, a gallon of water and a similar amount of lemonade. All the three of us could eat were two very small, shared plates of ratatouille. The girlfriend and the kids arrived late; but exhausted, we were happy to return home.

After Nicholas left, we moved to a small town called Georgioupolis and stayed at a hotel on the opposite end of the beach. There was a mountain stream that flowed into the sea, which was extremely cold at the point of egress, while the rest of the sea and the sand were hot. It was an amazing feeling just walking across the icy water of that stream. (I have only otherwise experienced that contrast in a creek in Guyana years later). One night too, we were at the restaurant cum dance place, when a pretty little Greek girl came to our table and asked Wolé to dance. She must have been three or four years older than Wolé, who was six years old. Wolé, who would not even dance with his sister, accepted. At one point, she left and went to the bathroom. On her return, she grabbed Wolé once again. He was dumbfounded, but complied. After that, he became a break-dancer. When we were on our way back to Brussels, Tanya who had decided to collect soda cans with Greek written on them, discovered that cans could take up quite a lot of baggage space and abandoned all her collection at the hotel.

Ronké visited once more and was lionised by two Dutch girls who insisted that she was one of the daughters in the Cosby show. They even asked their mother to allow them to stay with us for one day in which they tried to play tennis with Ronké. Ronké was a good player, having represented her school, Sidwell Friends, the best tennis school in the DC area. She also played with some of my friends and me. She played some beautiful left-handed inside out shots. Even at that level, she was competitive.

Thereafter, it was Wolé and my mother who visited together. We travelled to Venice and to Paris on different occasions. Venice did not seem as beautiful as when Harry and I had visited it en route to Asia Minor. But Mom also got to see the city after which she had been named, Verona. Wolé also visited once on his own, when Mom had gone to Kerala in Southern India (since I had been there). She was to sojourn at the house of the sister of a good friend in Barbados, Mohamed Muhajiri. Mom arrived at Kerala airport after having travelled alone from Maryland, to find no one waiting for her. Her hostess had been informed that the flight was two hours late. Not daunted, my mother went out to the taxi stand and asked if anyone knew the family she was visiting. In India, like in Barbados, houses do not normally have numbers and there are even fewer road signs. But one taxi driver knew and she arrived safely much to the astonishment of her hostess.

Wolé would get into the usual tussle with my housekeeper's daughter, who was about two years younger. They always had to play with the same toy or grab the same book; but they loved each other whenever they were not in a tussle.

This had all started when my housekeeper had brought her daughter to the Residence one Wednesday morning and indicated that her daughter wanted to have breakfast with me. She became like family. On Wednesdays, she would not go to kindergarten. She wanted to have breakfast with "der doctor" as she first called me, or "der Ambassador" as she later corrected herself. Her father was an administrator in the German Embassy and his wife Edith Fink worked as housekeeper at the Embassy Residence for several years before they were transferred to Cairo.

Much later, Mom, Wolé and I stayed with them when we visited Egypt. We were with a tour group and we saw the pyramids at Giza, the Cairo Museum, travelled up the Nile to the Valley of the Kings, Ramses' palace etc. The tour booked in Brussels, took us to the numerous sites of historic interest as well as sailing up the Nile to the Aswan dam. The tour guide knew precious little about the ancient Egyptians, as I learnt from later readings. The tour was fascinating nonetheless. On our way back to Brussels we stayed two days with the Finks. Now Wolé at 8 and Mary Jane at 6 were more sedate and talked peacefully. They kissed each other goodbye when we parted.

We also visited Stonehenge in Western England. I had asked Wolé what he knew about Stonehenge. He calmly replied: "Do you want to have the history or the myth?" We had to go to Stonehenge that summer. He was disappointed. He had believed that more of it was intact. It was however one of the better ruins we had seen anywhere. But that was a memorable tour. My mother who always enjoyed these outings was able to visit with her old friend, Vernon's ex-wife, Dr. Jane Yeo in Henley-on-Thames, but did not much like Oxford.

The most memorable visit was in 1990. I had been chosen as the Caribbean Representative to meet with Nelson Mandela on his first visit to Strasbourg. I opted to take Wolé and my mother along with me. As usual, we drove. Mom stayed at the hotel where we had a half-day stop, while I took along Wolé who was suitably dressed in suit and tie to the event. We arrived early so he took the opportunity to visit a rocket show, taking place at the same venue. After he had asked a number of very intelligent questions, he wanted to move on to the car show. The person responsible for the rocket show suggested that he wait until he could find the car expert, so informed had been Wolé's questions on rockets.

Then Mr. Mandela arrived. Wolé stood in the receiving line just before me. When Winnie Mandela came to him, he held out his hand in the usual fashion and she asked: "How is the youngest Ambassador?" The reply was a confident: "Fine, thank you Ma'am." Mr. Mandela then shook his hand with a very warm grip. He loved children. Both he and Mac Maraj said that what they had missed most on Robben Island was the voices and laughter of children.

When we returned to the hotel with a photo of Wolé speaking to Mrs. Mandela, Mom was waiting for us to report. Mandela himself then showed up, left the cortege and came over to Wolé and said: "Good to see you once again, young man." Mom said to Wolé that he might be too young to appreciate the occasion, but that that would be one of the most important meetings of his life. We received the photo of Wolé, who turned to me and said: "Dad, let's be cool about this. Don't tell everybody!" Of course when he returned to school in Maryland, he used the photo to indicate what he had done during his summer vacation. His fellow students did not believe him. They insisted it was a mock up of Mandela.

Apart from Belgium, I also covered other countries like Germany and Austria. One memorable visit to Berlin was on the occasion of a Trade Fair in that city. Normally, a rogue Honorary Consul we had in Northern Germany would turn up with gallons of Mount Gay rum punch, sell the lot and pocket the funds. He would more than cover the cost of attendance at the Fair. On this occasion, our more honest and proper Dr. Jens Schneiders, our Honorary Consul in Berlin, accompanied me. When the German Minister of Agriculture visited the Fair, the Northern gentleman attempted to monopolise the conversation with him. This had normally been possible since none of our previous Representatives, as far as I am aware, spoke German. I broke into the conversation and indicated that we did not only produce rum punch. Later, that gentleman attempted to claim the name Mount Gay in Germany. I recommended that he be dismissed. This, however, only happened when on one occasion his cows ate down someone else's field and he claimed (as one of our former Ambassadors had done for his dog) diplomatic immunity for the cows!

His success in selling rum punch indicated that we could have more than funded any visit to the Lisbon World Trade fair (when I was at CARICOM) and similarly at the Shanghai Fair. But we seem to learn rather slowly.

While most of my visits to Germany involved the matter of getting a Double Taxation Treaty with that country, I occasionally visited Vienna, Austria where we had a formidable Honorary Consul, Dr. Mack. Dr.

Mack and his wife took very good care of me and always tried to create opportunities for Barbados. My most memorable visit to Vienna was in 1993 for the Global Human Rights Conference. I prepared a tough speech, which Peter Laurie, then PS Foreign Affairs, approved. I naturally praised our efforts at securing the rights of all, but I hammered the Europeans and the USA who were inordinately self-righteous. I indicated that just a few years before the righteous folk from North-eastern Europe had been unfamiliar with the concept of human rights. I also pointed out to the US that not so long ago, a large segment of their populations did not have the right to vote, and that the African wars which they so magnified looked like a picnic as compared with what had been happening right where we were less than fifty years before. Naturally that speech did not go down well with the Europeans or the North Americans.

However, when I went down to the Drafting Committee, where no one could agree on a text, I wrote, in conjunction with a Trinidad and Tobago colleague what was the definitive compromise. I had left the Drafting Committee to return to the main hall. When I returned, the compromise was being incorporated into the final Declaration of the Conference. I had become once again the darling of the North and had retained my friendship with all members of the South.

Brussels was a continuum of trade talks and negotiations. I had constantly to deal with rum, sugar and the bananas and rice of other Caribbean countries. I recall that on one occasion when there was an impasse on some issue dealing with sugar, our sugar adviser from London, Anthony Murray, suggested that we mention the ecological importance of sugar to Barbados. The Minister was none too keen on the idea, but allowed me to proceed. I explained that we had very thin soil levels in Barbados and that we actually needed a grass covering to prevent wind erosion, and that sugar cane was the most suitable grass. It worked. The Europeans caved in and the Minister later, as Ministers often do, took the credit for the idea. As they say, victory has a thousand fathers. I would add that many of them have no legitimacy.

Brussels was also a place where information, not readily available elsewhere, could be garnered. Two issues come to mind: the genocide in Rwanda and the defeat of the apartheid fighters at Cuito Carnavale 111. The plane carrying both the President of Rwanda and that of Burundi had been shot down. The two presidents were returning from a meeting they had had with the Belgians. There was the almost instant beginning of a genocidal massacre. The UN troops were paralysed and the French troops secured French nationals and left the country to an immediate chaotic future.

I gathered from a letter I saw that the wife of the President had felt that he was surrendering the country to the Tutsi and that he was weak. According to the letter, she had conspired with a relative to have the plane shot down and that the act had been committed by two Martiniquan or Guadeloupean soldiers. A national radio station then set out on an ant-Tutsi campaign that ultimately left something like 800,000—Tutsi, the Canadian wife of a Minister, their children and Tutsi sympathisers—dead. The Commission called us in to discuss immediate assistance. The idea was to use unspent national funds to sort out the situation. Eventually, the situation in Rwanda was sorted out by the arrival of Tutsi troops from Uganda.

President Museveni (like my colleague and friend Charles Katungi) was also Ugandan Tutsi and had harboured in Western Uganda fighters from a previous massacre in Rwanda. They had helped him fight Milton Obote and had driven out the Tanzanians who wanted to seize power in Uganda and return that country to some near normalcy. The Rwandans who had fought with him now returned to their country to take on the murderers. Their leader, Paul Kagame, won and took over the country.

The second bit of information came from Botswana. It was about the beginning of the end of apartheid in Southern Africa. The apartheid South African Government had been helping Jonas Savimbi fight against the central Angolan Government. Savimbi (whom I met along with his 'Education Minister', whom he later had killed) was a ruthless psychotic personality. He controlled the diamonds of Eastern Angola and with earnings from these diamonds was able to wage a long war against the central government. He also had the support of the South

Africans (who considered any enemy of tranquillity in Southern Africa a friend of South Africa), as well as the USA.

The battle pattern had been consistent both in Cuito Carnavale I and II. The Angolans were however able to send a handful of their pilots to the Soviet Union and train them on the new Russian MIG 25's, clearly without the knowledge of the USA or the South Africans. What had happened in the first two battles at this small Southern Angolan town was that the Savimbi rebels and the Angolan troops would begin the battle, then the South African French-built Mirages would strafe the Angolan positions and the white elite South African troops would come into the battle to mop up.

On the occasion of Cuito Carnavale III, when the Mirages took to the sky, they were confronted by the superior MIGs, with their Angolan pilots speaking to each other in Russian to terrify the South Africans. Half the South African Air Force was shot down. The remaining half returned to base in what was to become Namibia. Namibians joined the Angolan forces, on this occasion, along with a large Cuban contingent now living in Angola as well as freedom fighters from elsewhere in South and Southern Africa. This combined force now encircled the white elite troops after killing several of them.

In the interim, news had somehow reached the general white population in South Africa that there had been several South African casualties and young white South

African males started burning their draft cards. The Defence Minister put out the falsehood that the South African troops had surrounded the Angolans. The President, however, had to agree to come to the table to discuss the return of his white troops. The Angolan terms were that Namibia would be given its independence and that South Africa would refrain from attacking its African neighbours. The US in the person of Ambassador Crocker demanded that the Cubans be expelled from Angola. The Angolans replied that they had Cubans who were now grandfathers in Angola. They accepted a reduced number of repatriations. The US and South African versions of the result of the Battle of Cuito Carnavale III differ slightly. Their legend is that the battle ended in a stalemate. This would hardly explain why the apartheid South African Government, which had resisted the UN mandate to free Namibia, would now suddenly agree both to Namibian independence as well as giving up the Caprivi Strip, a wedge of land between Botswana and Namibia which effectively controlled both countries. From this point onward, apartheid was slipping. What had begun as a small leak in the dam, became a torrent unstoppable by mere token concessions.

There was one other twist to the story. All of this occurred when Dame Nita was contesting Dante Caputo, a former Argentinian Foreign Minister for the Presidency of the UN. I had travelled with her to Addis Ababa to introduce her to the OAU Foreign Ministers who were to meet there. The Algerian Foreign Minister whom I had met and entertained in Barbados (with the help of my friend, Mohamed Muhajiri) was there. He came up to me, embraced me and asked what I needed. I explained to him. He promised to work this all out with his colleagues. We had proposed to travel to Cote d'Ivoire to speak to Ivoirian President, Houphet Boigny, but the Foreign Minister of Cote d'Ivoire made the call and informed us that the President had said that we could come to Abidjan if we wanted a vacation, but that he would certainly support the Barbados candidate.

Addis was in love with Dame Nita. Eight of my students from my Ghana days at the language institute were now interpreters (2) and translators (6) in the Organisation of African Unity. They came to ask me if they held a reception for Dame Nita whether she would come. I replied in the affirmative. They then said to me: "And you can come along too."

We returned, Dame Nita to New York where she was our Ambassador, and I to Brussels. This was precisely at the point where the South African Air Force was being pummelled. The French did not want to be directly involved in the replacement of the Mirage shells, but Argentina could. The Argentinians then promised the Francophone Africans all sorts of technical assistance if they supported Dante Caputo. The French joined in the arrangement. The 16 Francophone countries, which had been supportive of Dame Nita's candidacy, now went over to Caputo and the Argentinian won by 8 votes! What was ironic about this outcome was that Dame Nita's brother,

Errol Barrow had allowed Cuba to fly thousands of troops and ammunition into Angola before the US complained and the Prime Minister swore he knew nothing about it. His action had helped the Angolans, Cubans, Umkhonto we siswe et al defeat the South Africans. Having lost half their air force, they ultimately turned to Argentina, whose candidate defeated Dame Nita with more than a little help from Francophone Africa.

Brussels returned to its trade negotiations and its ACP-EU Joint Assembly meetings. The Joint Assembly meetings were meant to be meetings between European Parliamentarians and ACP Parliamentarians. However, several ACP countries were at that time dictatorships and they therefore had no parliamentarians in the sense of elected members of parliament. Their Ambassadors thus usually represented them. The members of the European Parliament did not all like this. Nonetheless the meetings took place all over the ACP countries including Papua New Guinea and in Brussels or Strasbourg. I had persuaded Prime Minister Sandiford to let Dr. Erskine Simmons be a permanent representative for Barbados. This would give him a chance to learn the system and therefore put the Barbados position forcefully.

To his credit, Dr. Simmons did learn the system quickly and well. Thus when the ACP Presidency became vacant, I put up his name and he was elected without his even knowing it. He was delighted, promised that in his radio/television programme, he would let Barbados know what the Embassy had achieved. He never did. We therefore travelled to meetings in Papua New Guinea, in Congo and there was one special meeting in Barbados, where I could show off what we, small country that we were, had. The British media had a field day. The European Parliament was off on a junket, they argued. Who could be going to Barbados to conduct an ACP-EU political session? One of the main points of discussion at the Barbados session turned out to be bananas. Dame Eugenia held forth although the advice to her was to seek to diversify within or out of bananas.

However, the Europeans had a great time as did my African and Pacific colleagues. Charles Katungi, Josh Iroha and I had lunch at Richard Armstrong's little restaurant in Queen's Park. They both enjoyed it to the point that when Josh returned sometime later to a meeting in Grenada, he stopped off in Barbados, took a taxi to the park and ate once more at the restaurant. Josh, Charles and Richard have now joined the ancestors. Both Charles and Richard died of ruptured aneurisms in the brain. Josh was a chain smoker and I do not imagine that his posting to Liberia during the civil war there did much for his health.

There was one incident, which said something very clearly about our literacy. We were travelling on a bus tour. There was a man along the Black Rock road sweeping the streets. When we returned, it was his lunch hour, so he was sitting, reading a newspaper. One of my African colleagues was surprised. In his country, no one who could read and probably write would be a street cleaner! I also developed a close friendship with the Ambassador of Gabon, a light-skinned African who had always been mistaken in Paris, where he had studied, for someone from Martinique or Guadeloupe.

They were usually disappointed when he could speak no creole. He enjoyed Barbados. He wanted to get hold of the calypso *Columbus Lie* and some Bajan rum. I got him a case of old rum, which he took with him on the plane and kept on his lap! He continued also to sing *Columbus Lie*. Regrettably, on his return to Brussels, he broke with the Brussels Francophone clique within the ACP. They complained to his Foreign Minister (the Ivorian Ambassador had evidently once been a Minister) and he was recalled.

France was in the habit of summoning the Francophones to a meeting just before any ACP-EU Council Meeting. Katungi, Iroha and I cooked up the idea that we should ask the UK Minister, Christopher Patton to invite us to a meeting in London. It had to be on a Tuesday or Thursday, when we normally held Ambassadorial meetings. He did. The Dean of the ACP Ambassadors, the Representative of Mauritius, which like the Seychelles were bilingual, began to report on the consultation in London. The Francophones were worried that the British had now entered the game, and the Mauritian Ambassador was doing nothing to change their belief that the British had summoned us to London. At this point, Iroha got up and said that he had got it all wrong. We—and he mentioned the names—had asked for the meeting and had decided on which day it was to be held!

◎

Dr. Simmons had served his term as President of the ACP Parliamentarians. The Francophone clique now wanted to hold the post. We could have won in an open election, so effective and popular was Dr. Simmons, but that would have burnt any bridges between the Francophones, and us. I therefore recommended that he surrender the post. He did so graciously, but proceeded on his return to Barbados to complain that I had sold him down the river! I was extremely disappointed.

We had conducted a joint human rights mission to Malawi to persuade President Banda to release some political detainees. The Malawians had even flown in the detainees to talk to us. We did get an opportunity too to speak to the President directly. We discovered that he was an erudite old man whose office had been virtually controlled by one of his Ministers and his personal secretary. He spoke about the Roman occupation of Portugal and how ultimately that brutal occupation became reflected in the Portuguese treatment of its colonised peoples.

The Malawians were also gracious and flew us by helicopter to Lake Malawi, the deepest lake in the world. The Malawians had discovered oil beneath the lake, but had no intentions of disturbing the lake and its environment, where, for instance, the tilapia, a particularly ravenous fish elsewhere, did not bother other species, over 600 in number. The women who sold fish on the beach also explained why there were no flies to be seen anywhere. They said that when the fish were laid out in a specific way toward the sun, the flies were not attracted. We also flew over a river that flowed into the lake and saw hippos wrestling and otherwise playing down below.

Soon after we had left, Dr. Banda died and the regime fell apart. It was interesting that Dr. Banda had been among the future southern African leaders that Kwame Nkrumah had hosted before their country became independent, but Dr. Banda was the only one to make an accord with apartheid South Africa. It was in some ways fitting that he died before the fall of apartheid in that country.

My human rights missions in Africa were not ended. Much later, when I was elected out of turn, the ACP Ambassadorial Chairman, I accompanied the ACP Secretary General, Edwin Carrington, on a mission to Djibouti along with inter alia, two Parliamentarians from Suriname. We toured the area and went to the border of Somalia to look at the problems of health etc., encountered by the nomadic peoples of the area. The problem was that the nomadic herdsmen of Djibouti would come to the hospital with tuberculosis and leave before they were totally cured. This spread the tuberculosis virus in a somewhat stronger version to other nomads, and curing the new disease was considerably more difficult.

Carrington, who spoke French, but evidently became shy, asked me to reply to the host's speech in French. I complied. The women responded with the usual ululating sounds of approval.

My human rights career had begun much earlier with my attendance at a UPR in Geneva. I attended on behalf of Barbados. I worked with Geraldine Ferraro, the head of the US delegation as they thought Barbados was a good fit for their views. Indonesia did not much approve since we refused to support them on East Timor.

Later, a problem arose in Gabon. Evidently a group of undocumented immigrants from neighbouring countries and Nigeria had entered Gabon without crossing any established border post. They were caught and detained in a large open area with a shed. The rain came and the guards moved them into the shed and, out of fear that they would escape, closed the shed. It was mercilessly hot inside and several of the detainees died. When word of this came, the European Parliament described this as a gross violation of human rights. We agreed to send a delegation to Gabon. The Secretary General, then the Ethiopian, Mr. Birhane, did not want to go, so I, as Chairman of the Committee of ACP Ambassadors headed the Mission. We got to meet President Bongo, a small man and a dictator. He was quite affable and explained what had happened. It was, however, Foreign Minister Ping, to whom I made some suggestions. I felt that since what had happened was more an error of judgement than a deliberate violation of human rights, the President should sack the Minister responsible, sack the guards and pay some form of compensation. Mr. Ping found this acceptable. The Minister was moved to another post and the guards were duly sacked, and Mr. Ping came to Brussels to explain the situation before the European Parliament. The situation was thus resolved.

One final European Parliament session brought up the matter of the treatment of the Tuareg in Mali. The Malians had brought a delegation, which included about five different ethnic groups in their parliament, including a Tuareg in full regalia. The Tuareg had traditionally been a nomadic, horse and camel riding people who attacked the riverine peoples, enslaving them and making them produce food and women for them, inter alia. The countries of Mali, Niger and Chad wanted the Tuareg to adopt one nationality or the other and not move uncontrolled from one country to the other. A member of the Green party took up the Tuareg cause, without of course understanding the issue. When someone asked if she was defending the Tuareg merely because of their lighter skin colour, she cried openly. The matter therefore ended there.

Perhaps my signal human rights achievement was at the Global Conference on Human Rights in Vienna in 1993. I was the sole representative of Barbados and therefore had to be in Plenary some of the time and in the Drafting Committee whenever possible. In the Plenary there was a barrage of speeches by Western and Eastern Europeans and the North Americans extolling their democracies, and decrying the various conflicts that existed at the time. In my turn, I explained how a small country like Barbados maintained its democratic norms, but that I was unable to understand the bombast, when democracy was a bad word in some Northern Countries five years before, and in one country only 35 years ago, a large segment of its citizenship did not even have the right to vote. With respect to war, what was occurring at the moment was like a picnic compared to what raged in Europe fifty years before. This made me persona non grata with the West, but allowed me access among the Third World countries. The result was that when I went to the Drafting Committee and there was an impasse, together with my colleague from Trinidad and Tobago, I was able to draft wording that all delegations accepted and it made both the purveyors of bombast and those on the defensive appreciative.

Towards the end of my stay in Brussels, I became involved with negotiations leading to the establishment of the World Trade Organisation. The WTO was a huge step forward. Before it emerged, the GATT, its predecessor, was nothing more than a rich countries' club. They made decisions in the Green Room and the rest of the world was forced to obey. However, with the arrival of Brazil, India and China on to the world stage there were other big countries that Europe and the USA had to deal with: hence the ultimate agreement came into being, setting up the WTO. Nonetheless, the Brussels meeting continued along a familiar pattern. They were preparing to do a deal using tropical agriculture as the ultimate victim of a trade deal. A BBC journalist asked me what I thought of the whole process. I replied with the African proverb, which says that when elephants do battle, it is the grass that suffers. I explained that we in the small third world countries were the grass. He returned later for another comment and I respectfully suggested that there was a Jamaican Minister around and he might wish to speak to that Minister.

That was during my last year in Brussels. The ACP elected me out of turn to lead the negotiations with the EU for Lomé V. On the EU side, their lead speaker at the Ambassadorial level was a Mr. Pooley, who was in the habit of making fun of his ACP counterparts. Sadly, he tried the same tactic with me, and each time he made some joke, I responded with a better one. He would say something like: "When I have been in the Caribbean, I have had to show my passport in each country where I arrive, while in Europe, I never need to." I had to remind him that the Caribbean was made up largely of islands and that the airports catered for all sorts of people coming from anywhere! He also suggested that the ACP-EU Joint Assembly should be once a year to allow for genuine elected politicians to attend. There could be some special funding for such an Assembly. I asked whether this was a solid promise or just some old talk. It turned out to be, as we say, just a lot o' long talk.

Since Pooley was constantly forced to return to serious discussion, the negotiations went smoothly until it moved to the ministerial level. The former Ambassador of Senegal was now Senegal's Foreign Minister. Evelyn Greaves, the Barbados Minister of Trade was the Barbados Ministerial Representative. As usual, the French came up with an offer of a sum to fund the relationship. The Senegalese approached Minister Greaves to suggest that it was now time to end the negotiations by accepting the French offer. Our Minister replied: "Is that an acquis (a given)?"

In this period, I went to Swaziland as Chairman of the ACP Ambassadors. When elected, I informed the Minister of the victory for Barbados. He inquired what it would cost Barbados. He was the same Minister who had declared that buying a building in New York, which could possibly now be paying for the Barbados Foreign Service had no political constituency.

The EU/ACP now paid for all my official travel expenses. I also had special status at all meetings, and was given a driver. This allowed me to visit a former colleague from Swaziland during an ACP/EU meeting there. Arrived at his house, I commenced the walk up his 50-metre long driveway and almost froze. It was about 3 degrees Celsius! So much for the myth of Africa being burning hot!

While I was in Swaziland, my mother fell ill. Dr. Jillian Marville, my cousin, telephoned the Embassy to pass on the information, and in the process reached me in Swaziland. I asked as much as I could. It seemed that my mother had liquid under her heart and they were afraid that it might be cancerous. I called the hospital and reached the doctor in charge. He naturally asked my mother what I was doing in Swaziland. She answered proudly that her son was the Barbados Ambassador in Brussels and that he was probably in Swaziland chairing some meeting. There I was, worried about her and she was casually boasting about her son. She recovered, but stopped working at that point. She was 75.

When the second part of the negotiations resumed, the Francophones whose turn it was, insisted on taking over the Presidency. I would not have minded except that it was one of my least forceful colleagues and Pooley ran all over her. This, however, gave me a chance to finish my MBA at the European University in Brussels. I had done one third of the course work one summer when I had taken vacation. I was thus able to finish it well before I left Brussels.

Studying required incredible organisation. I would leave work and go directly to classes between 6 and 9 pm, go home, sleep for a few hours, wake up and read, then sleep for another few hours before preparing for work once again. Inevitably, I still woke up in the middle of the night at the weekend. There was a French programme with a very catchy classical tune that accompanied a short film of half an hour. I watched and enjoyed that and went back to sleep, this time, until morning.

There was a change of Government in Barbados and the new Foreign Minister came to Brussels. She wanted to have a meeting of the Caribbean Group, which had to be held in the Residence. I had identified a suitable building for the Embassy in an area where there was another Embassy and a park in front of the site. It had been designed and built by an architect. He and his wife were getting divorced and he was being forced to sell the house cheaply. I arranged with Foreign Affairs and the Finance Ministry to purchase the property. Peter Laurie wrote constantly to the Ministry of Finance, but the PS there would never respond on paper. Snide remarks about Marville's house were about the best that could be garnered. We had paid down 20% of the cost, but when after a year we had failed to make any arrangement for the full payment, the Government of Barbados lost that 20% and any claim to be able to purchase the property.

We subsequently had, in the early nineties, to close off the lower entrances to the Residence and use the top floor for the Embassy. This process meant that when the new Minister arrived, we had to find new ways of hosting her.

The new Minister arrived. I now had an offer from Edwin Carrington, who had become Secretary-General of CARICOM to take up the post of Assistant Secretary General to deal with the body's Foreign and Internal Relations. The Caribbean Group met in the drawing room of the Residence. It was a rather cosy affair. My new Filipina housekeeper, Marietta, had learnt how to make various Bajan dishes from my mother. With a little help from my very efficient Secretary, Gaile Thompson, a Caribbean style buffet was on offer. One of my colleagues even asked who catered for me. He was stunned to hear that my staff had done it all. In the room, I had occasionally to translate from French and Spanish, which was not part of my job.

The meeting went well. I informed the Minister that I had had an offer that I wanted to take up. I wanted to go home. I had been in Brussels for eight years. She asked me to stay on for another year. I indicated that Michael King or Errol Humphrey would make excellent replacements. Although she then appointed Michael and later Errol, she never forgave me for refusing her. She commented that the reception had been simple but elegant. She made no comment on the fact that I had had to interpret for the Haitian and Dominicano delegates. She seemed only concerned about my wishing to leave. Some people can be extremely vindictive and silly.

The long Brussels experience was particularly useful in terms of my diplomatic career. As a bonus, I had made some very good friends. Apart from Charles Katungi and Josh Iroha, there was Charles Savarin of Dominica, who later became a Minister and then President of that country. The Fijian Ambassador with whom I discussed Fijian origins and whose beautiful country I visited later became their Foreign Minister. I later set up a joint venture between the R.L. Seale rum factory and the one in Fiji. The deal was all but done. The idea was to have R.L. Seale produce Barbados rum in Fiji, expressly for the Australian market. It was almost done when the Australians came in and bought out the Fijian factory. David Seale graciously praised the effort of the Embassy on his return.

I also made one very good friend who was to be my mate on and off for the next several years. Indeed, the relationship, moribund since Fiji, was rekindled in Swaziland and continued into my sojourn at CARICOM. She was a delegate for Suriname at all the ACP-EU Council meetings. She, Ollye Chin-a-Sen, was a senior economist and a very beautiful woman. We shared a household in Georgetown where I next went and where she orchestrated a job with her airline.

Brussels was a great situation for entertainment both in terms of accommodation and utility, but the small staff and the work-load did not make for much general entertaining, although I did entertain the local Bajan community separately, Professor Cardinal Warde together with the diplomatic staff etc. On the other occasion where I entertained a large gathering, I had received a box of flying fish from Barbados and I invited the Chef de Cabinet of the European President and a number of my colleagues, including the Ambassador of Cameroon and the Charge d'Affaires of Haiti. I did the cooking. When they complimented my housekeeper, she informed them that I had done it myself.

On that occasion I got to advertise our old rum. The Chef de Cabinet of the European President, Ambassador Daniel Martin, started the hilarity of the evening when he arrived with two of my female colleagues and a third said to him; "You have a beautiful wife." Daniel casually inquired "Which one?" After dinner, I suggested that he should try our rum. He scoffed at the idea initially, but then smelled the old rum. "This is not rum," he said. I informed him that it was not his rum (Martiniquan rhum). I suggested that he was all too familiar with French cognacs and armagnacs and that he should perhaps try our rum. He did and he later had a second glass. What's more, he turned up one evening just to have a chat. I offered him a drink. At first he refused. Then he accepted and had six shots of old rum. I must thank the Goddards for always keeping me in good supply. Daniel then took a taxi back home.

Georgetown

WHEN I informed Ollye that I would be going to Georgetown to work at the CARICOM Secretariat as Assistant Secretary General with responsibility for Foreign and Internal Affairs, she was pleased. I would be at least close to Suriname. She informed me that the Head of Suriname Airways had once said to her that he would be happy to offer her a job. We went to see him. She said that she was ready to accept the job he constantly offered. She wanted to be in Georgetown. He made her Head of a Georgetown Office, which was to be responsible for all Caribbean flights. She accepted and we went looking for a house to rent. We eventually found more or less what we wanted on Rupununi Street in Belair Park, just off Vlessingen Road.

My job in CARICOM was to look after the member states' foreign policy interests in so far as they could be co-ordinated or did not conflict with each other. It meant, inter alia, preparing the agenda for the foreign policy aspect of Heads of Government meetings as well as for ACP Heads' meetings and Foreign Ministers meetings. It also meant that if a CARICOM Head of Government was designated to visit an ACP country, for instance, I might be asked to accompany him to provide instant background. This also extended to important events within CARICOM, like the opening of the Surinamese ferry to Guyana or negotiating an accession treaty with Haiti.

I also attended CARICOM-CUBA summits. Fidel Castro was always in attendance and made long, rambling but passionate speeches that seemed to be in the mode of a campaigning politician. He was never dull. In one meeting in Port-of Spain, the steel band in attendance gave a fabulous rendering of Handel's Hallelujah chorus. When asked about it, he said he adored it, but that there was not much to sing Hallelujah for in Cuba. On one occasion in Havana, I met both Fidel and Teofilo Stevenson, the legendary Cuban boxer, who indicated that he had met Mohammed Ali and that they were friends. In a conversation with Fidel, who was not a short man, he was surprised at the height of two of my colleagues, one of whom was from Anguilla. I informed him that Anguilla had been used as a breeding station. He seemed not to have known that, so I asked if he had assumed that Hitler had performed the first attempt at selective breeding.

Almost all travel out of Georgetown began at about three a.m. Trinidad was our real hub. This was fine, since I often travelled with Ollye or on one occasion, I even happened to be there when she was also at work with some of her colleagues there. There had been some problem with the airline and we, the passengers, were put up at the Holiday Inn, where she also was. At first I stayed in her room, since her colleagues might call to speak to her, but there was so much noise there that we switched to my room on the other wing of the hotel.

What had brought me there on that occasion was rather strange. We had arrived at Piarco Airport when we heard that someone had stolen the copper wire connecting the lighting system at the Airport outside Georgetown. The question was whether they could find a set of lights the airport authorities could borrow to facilitate the landing of an aircraft. It was clear to me that this was a futile effort. We sat on the plane. I informed the stewardess that I felt like a hostage and I wanted to leave the plane. She responded that there was no ground flight attendant to escort me off. I was sitting next to the Guyanese Foreign Minister. I insisted that the flight attendant pass my message on to the pilot.

The pilot informed her that I could alight if I so wanted. So I did and went to the First Class lounge and had something to eat and drink. Eventually, I was informed that the other passengers were alighting in a few minutes, so I returned to collect my briefcase. A young man with a very thin voice was trying to make an announcement. No one could hear him, so I took over and asked everyone to listen. They were informed that there would be buses to take everyone to the Holiday Inn. I could see only three or four small buses around, so I asked whether First Class passengers were not entitled to an individual taxi. A positive response came immediately. I then announced that I was prepared to take three people with me in my taxi. I believe other passengers followed my lead so we all arrived safely at the Holiday Inn. When we returned to the airport for a 7 a.m. flight to Georgetown, the Foreign Minister had already departed by an earlier flight.

On one of the accompaniment treks, I went with the Prime Minister of Dominica to Zimbabwe. I had been to Zimbabwe a few times before. On one such occasion, a Zimbabwean Minister thanked us for the scholarships that Barbados had provided a few Zimbabweans at UWI. He indicated that that had allowed them to place two indigenous Zimbabweans in positions in the public Service, after the ouster of Ian Smith, the former racist dictator of that country.

Zimbabwe is possibly the most beautiful country I have ever seen. It has three climates: the southern lowlands where they grow sugar cane, mangoes and other tropical crops, the central veldt, where they grow wheat etc., and the eastern highlands where they grow apples, pears et al.

That apart, about 100 kilometres outside the capital Harare is Great Zimbabwe, the old Shona city that stands in impressive ruin, but still with a cylindrical tower, the remnants of the royal palace, from which when the Monomotopa spoke, he could be heard a kilometre away down in the city. There are other zimbabwes (stone cities) scattered around in Zimbabwe itself and even into what is now South Africa and Botswana. It must have been a formidable empire in its day, trading as far afield as China and maintaining some of the symbols of power that date back to Kemet (ancient Egypt). It was at one point considered a Portuguese settlement, since, according to Eurocentric myth, Africans were not supposed to have been able to create anything like that. Later, when the South Africans did a dig there, they could only find what they called 'kaffir stuff'.

Zimbabwe also has one of the most exciting physical features in the world, Mosi-oa-tunya, the Victoria Falls. It is the largest falls in the world. The falls are in fact in neighbouring Zambia, but can only properly be seen from the southern side of the Zambezi River, in Zimbabwe. It also has in a park near Harare remnants of old San paintings along with another natural phenomena, the hanging rocks. These enormous boulders seem to have been the result of erosion, which has left huge rocks perched on top of each other in the uncanniest balance.

As if that were not enough for one country, Zimbabwe also has a large lake on the Zambezi, created by a dam built further down the river. There are islands on the lake, which provide both leisure in the form of sailing, and fish for food. The sad thing about the country is that the man who created its democracy was to become the man who destroyed both that democracy and the economy of the country, to some extent with the connivance of the UK and the USA.

CARICOM was not the organisation I had known under Willie Demas and Alistair McIntyre. Edwin Carrington, who was more interested in photo-ops than in any broad new Caribbean policies, was leading it. He would always side with any criticism of his staff rather than defending his colleagues. Two examples came immediately to mind. I was asked to attend a meeting in Jamaica on cricket. The Regional Heads of Government had decided that they would put some money into West Indies cricket, which was now faltering. I attended the Meeting where the Head of the Board outlined a proposal, which he indicated would make money. I asked the perfectly reasonable question as to why it was necessary to ask Governments for money when a money-making venture could be handled by private investment. He complained to Carrington, who ensured that I would never attend such a meeting again. So the Secretariat continued to trot out bureaucratic documents on cricket. These basically said that the Heads had decided so and so. No real proposal was then put forward. I was virtually banished from cricket until there was to be a match between the Heads (which also included the Secretariat and Joel Garner) versus the University, which included David Holford etc.

I bought a new bat, but had little opportunity to practise. Furthermore, Prime Minister Arthur, who talks a good game, borrowed my bat and edged one to the wicketkeeper and was out for 1 run. Oddly, the first ball I faced was from Dr. Hilary Beckles. It was a half volley and some memory device kicked in and I smacked it to the mid off boundary. He glared at me, but that did not faze me. I went on to make 40 not out. Garner and the Prime Minister of Grenada also made some runs. Interestingly, when the University batted, Beckles made 50 not out, but they did not reach our score. It was not David Holford's day. He made a duck after he had been duly carted around the place by all and sundry.

After that match, everybody realised that I did know something about the game and my counsel was once again sought. This time it was about Brian Lara's captaincy. I wrote quite bluntly that Lara was more interested in batting, where he was more than competent and should not be burdened with the captaincy. Needless to say, such advice was discarded and the memorandum began with the usual reference to what the last Heads Meeting had decided etc.

The second incident was when the Trinidad and Tobago delegate complained about the lack of documents in some area dealing with Foreign Affairs. I said that as Head of that section, I accepted the criticism, but I had to remind delegates that my entire Section contained 9 persons including secretaries, so there was bound to be some slip ups. The Economics Section said that it was noticeable that Marville stood up for members of his staff, but that some other Heads did not. One of my most diligent officers also added publicly that Ambassador Marville was the only person in the Secretariat who cared about her two small sons. That made me doubly at fault.

CARICOM involved endless travel throughout the Region as well as in Europe and Africa. It even involved meetings in Tokyo, where the Japanese arrogance showed its face. When the Secretary General could not attend one of the meetings and I had to chair, the Japanese considered it unworthy to have an Assistant Secretary General chair, even though they had the participation of Ambassador Sydney Poitier in support of my chairmanship. I had actually attended a meeting prior to that one. The Secretary General had chaired it. In any event, the Region obtained precious little from Japan.

They took us on a trip across the main island to visit a nuclear plant. I asked whether it was safe, since Japan is one of the countries on the so-called ring of fire. They naturally swore that it was totally safe. A more recent incident proved them wrong, but then arrogance is often associated with that sort of stance. Tokyo was a murderously expensive, but clean and well-ordered city. We happened to return to Tokyo at rush hour with some two million persons coming out of the central station with the rapidity and order that I would only otherwise expect in China. I was otherwise disappointed in Japan, which seemed interested merely in granting scholarships for students wanting to learn Japanese culture.

The worse connection to Japan was that they acquired spent nuclear fuel from France. This was then shipped to Japan via the Caribbean Sea. Any suggestion of an accident would have damaged our tourism. Any real accident, however apparently trivial, would have ruined fish stock in the Region and ruined tourism for decades. We were later, as a pan-Caribbean group to protest this shipment route. Even the delegate from Martinique, a French Departement, joined in the protest.

It also involved travel to Africa for ACP-EU Council

Meetings like the one in Gabon. There I went with Prime Minister Arthur and his Jamaican wife to the local market. I also remember going to a lobster restaurant, where the lobster served was so large that I could not finish the meal I had ordered.

We also ran a Trade Mission to South Africa, where I came into conflict with the Secretary General once again. I wanted to have a Barbadian consultant who was prepared to conduct the entire operation. The SG insisted on a Trinidadian group who offered a more limited set of services to be supplemented by a local Guyanese businessman. At one point in the process, there were some glitches. The Guyanese did not show up. Naturally, he blamed me, not in my presence, but in front of the business people who had gone on the trek. The Barbadian contingent simply informed me later. Because of the several persons responsible for different roles, the operation was a total failure.

There were some areas where there was more success. I negotiated the entry of Haiti into CARICOM. Although it was understood that the language of communication for Haiti within CARICOM was English, the Haitian delegation was more comfortable with the occasional conversation in French. After several sessions both in Georgetown and Port-au-Prince, we came up with an agreement where Haiti's entry would be conditional on there being a free and fair election to the Haitian Senate in the upcoming elections. I also travelled to Haiti to explain to a group of Haitian businessmen the mechanisms of

CARICOM trade.

Interestingly, Aristide was comfortable with the goings-on. The Caribbean Representatives in Brussels had after all given him great support and it did seem that he had been pushed out of the Presidency by the military, still unwilling to see Haiti become a democracy. We were yet to realise that Bertrand Aristide, once a poor parish priest, but now married to a mulatte lawyer was en route to being a repeat of Papa Doc.

There was a memorable Heads of Government Summit in Suriname. They were doing repairs in the hotel where I was staying and I lost my voice. This resulted in the absurd situation of the SG having to read my contribution to that meeting. Then there was a retreat far away from Paramaribo where each delegation was allowed two members, usually the Prime Minister or President and his Foreign Minister. The Secretariat was allowed four members. I was one of the four. Prime Minister Arthur asked the Secretary General if there were any structural changes he would want to see. Even with the voice of Sir Sridath calling for the sort of reform of the system into something approaching the European Commission, the SG could only say that all was well.

There were a few memorable incidents in Guyana itself. I found a book on possible sites for a hydroelectric dam in Guyana. I discussed the idea with the late Minister of Trade. He was excited and proposed that we meet with the President, Sam Hinds, who happened to be an engineer. We did, with the Minister pushing for the idea.

I had also indicated that the Japanese could be asked to provide a turnkey operation, which they would fund on very generous terms. The President said the dam would produce too much electricity! "We would have an excess of too many megawatts," he said. With Georgetown without streetlights and most factories and homes relying on generators, this was a surprising response to a plant that would have supplied maybe ten megawatts more than was immediately needed. Now nearly twenty years later, Guyana is embarking on or discussing a hydroelectric project.

Ollye often travelled with me on meetings. She travelled anywhere within the Region on an ID 100, which meant that as long as there was an available seat, she could travel. I could easily accommodate her. It was common knowledge that we lived together in what was acceptable Surinamese style. Of course, whenever there was a meeting in Suriname itself, she could find a work related reason for travelling to Paramaribo. Also, on occasion, when I had a few days free, we would travel there and stay in the house of her parents. I liked her father and would take him Bajan rum or milk from the Pine Hill Dairy, both of which he enjoyed.

She also arranged a trip for the CARICOM Secretariat staff up the Koppername River to a Maroon settlement. This was an event in itself. We travelled upriver in a dugout of the sort that had long been used by Africans and the Kalina (miscalled Caribs) who travelled in such boats up to fifty persons at a time and who gave us the word canoe.

One member of our party, a female lawyer, was terrified. I once looked back to speak to someone and she interjected: "No, do not look back." She was afraid that I would topple over the boat. Those boats had traditionally carried up to fifty strong Kalinago (male Kalina soldiers) quite easily.

Arrived at a Maroon village, we saw children swimming in the river near the pier where we landed. We were presented to the chief, who, in proper Akan style, had a linguist through whom we addressed him. We were shown one of the houses with its collection of objets d'art. We were then treated to a lunch, like one we would have had in Ghana, of rice and chicken cooked in a peanut sauce. It was delicious and probably meant more to me than any of my colleagues.

Relations with Ollye were never perfect when her parents were with us, except when we were in Barbados. Her father loved cricket. He would travel to Barbados or Guyana to watch Test cricket. When we were doing rather badly against Australia, thanks partly to a catch picked up off the ground by Waugh to dismiss Brian Lara, he wanted to go back home. It was my job to persuade him to stay for another week. He also got to meet his cricketing idol, Sir Garry. I arranged a meeting at the Golf Club in the centre of the island and he was delighted. However, outside of Barbados, Ollye seemed to need to show her parents that she was in control. In their absence we got on extremely well. Somehow, it was clear that she would not entertain the thought of setting up a household away from her parents. Thus, after my Haitian stint, where she visited and even joined me on helicopter visits to the countryside, we saw each other less often and things began to fall apart.

Before that we stayed with my mother in Maryland; my son stayed with us in Georgetown and Mom visited in Georgetown as well as accompanying me once on a Christmas visit to Suriname, where we stayed in Ollye's apartment on the floor above her father's business in the heart of the city.

Mom enjoyed these visits and even made a special friend in Parika, a small market town on the Essequibo River, Guyana. It is a long drive by Caribbean standards from Georgetown to Parika. It involves crossing the bridge over the Demerara River and travelling along the townships that lie on the river all the way across country to Parika. All the dykes on the river fascinated Mom.

Arrived at Parika, we were walking along the small roadway that separated stalls in the marketplace. Out came a woman from her stall and embraced my mother as if they had known each other for years. Mom also returned the embrace. It was evident to me that they had known each other in a former incarnation. Mom somehow accepted this even though it contradicted her very orthodox religious beliefs. Whenever we went back to Parika, we visited her friend. If she did not have what we were looking for, she would scour the market for it on our behalf. When Mom was not there, she would offer to send her some limes or other goodies that could not be shipped to the USA. When Mom returned, she would bring her friend T-shirts or other knick-knacks that she appreciated.

The frequent visits to Parika made me curious about life further up the river and so I ventured to Bartika and a small island near Bartika on the Essequibo River. I liked it enough to schedule a visit by representatives on Foreign Affairs from the various member states. We had always met in the sterile setting of the Secretariat before. Everyone was delighted to venture upriver. Travelling to the island in the late evening was an interesting experience. Someone thought that lights in the distance were the other side of the river as distinct from an island in the river that they were.

During the meeting, the representative of Dominica said: "We believe in Dominica that we have 365 rivers, but I am going to have to tell my Prime Minister that we have no rivers at all." The Guyanese delegate boasted that there was an island near the mouth of the river as large as Barbados. This is not true, as the island in question is not even 100 square miles. I had the same notion repeated to me on one occasion by the Guyanese Foreign Minister. I simply asked him what the GNP of the island was, and that more or less settled the issue.

I was seldom in Georgetown. When I was not away at some ACP-EU Meeting, there was no end of meetings within the Region. One of the more memorable series was in Montserrat. The volcano in the south of the island had exploded. Erupted is not quite the word. It destroyed the entire capital city and left a small strip of volcanically formed land offshore. Several people were consumed by the magma and just about all property in the city was destroyed. One resident described how on returning to his old house he realised that lava had come through the roof landed in the toilet bowl, obliterated it and left a huge hole in the ground. Life on the island had to be shifted northward—and there is not much available land north of the capital. Some residents moved to Antigua and a few fled to the United Kingdom. There was a great need for immediate rebuilding elsewhere on the island.

CARICOM was justifiably of the view that the UK should bear the brunt of the rebuilding process, since Montserrat was and is a dependency of the UK. The problem was that the UK would have preferred all the inhabitants to desert the island either in favour of living in the UK or possibly elsewhere in the Region. Montserrat could then become a military base for the UK in the Caribbean. It therefore became something of a fight for the British to accept their responsibility and provide permanent housing in a suitable area, far from the area of the volcano.

This eventually happened. All the while, a group of seismologists monitored activity in the volcano, indicating when it was safe to return to the area. A handful of people ignored the danger warnings on one occasion and suffered the ultimate loss. However, the smallest member of CARICOM, a British dependency returned to some form of normalcy in time.

One other major project that we worked on was the

matter of CARICOM representation in the form of joint Missions. Our first target was South Africa. Briefly, we worked out a method of rotation that would serve to change the Ambassador along state lines with representation from all countries present to an extent and with the Ambassador representing the interests of all countries. It seemed like a good idea until Trinidad and Tobago had reservations. In the interim, the Trinidad and Tobago Government changed political hands. The same person remained as Foreign Minister, but he claimed that there was not enough information! My most senior officer, who had personally worked on the detail, offered him a dossier about 300 pages long. It made no difference other than to highlight one of the fundamental difficulties of CARICOM. Even within countries, there can be a shift in policy for no other reason that one can adduce but that the new government wants to follow a new, but unnamed, path.

One other area of travel was to the United Nations. There I visited my old friends from Roosevelt Island. It was in the wind that Kofi Annan was going to be elected Secretary General of the United Nations. So I congratulated him. He modestly suggested that no one had so informed him. Later when he had become Secretary General, I told him that I could not then congratulate him, since I had done so months before. He laughed in his very gentle way.

On that later visit, I was reminded of what I did not like about New York. It was still the dirtiest major city

I had ever visited. It still made one pay for whatever was in scarce supply. Ollye joined me there. When she came up to the room, which was expensive, she asked whether there was not another room. Later in the stay, it was raining and we hailed a taxi. As soon as the cab arrived, a man jumped in front of us and got into the taxi.

CARICOM was not great for my health. There were several problems. Guyana is not blessed with multiple airline services, and where services do exist, they represent the end of the line. Thus, unless one is travelling to Suriname or simply, say, to Trinidad or Barbados, flights have to begin at 6.00 am. Given the distance from the city to the airport, it meant waking at 3.00 am to be picked up by the shuttle. One was constantly tired when travelling. I ended up on one occasion with cancer, which has been in remission ever since it was treated in Sweden, and hepatitis, which had to be treated in Barbados, since no one wanted to be in the hospital in Georgetown at the time.

I was shuttled weak to Bridgetown to be treated by my old friend, Professor Mickey Walrond. After I had been declared fit again, he advised that I should have another week before returning to work and indicated that I could stay at his house if I promised to relax during that time. I did in fact relax. My only entertainment was on evenings when his wife Beverley returned home. She was handling a bizarre legal case and she kept me au fait with the developments from day to day. It was like a soap opera. Suitably recuperated, I returned to Georgetown. I was to serve the last extended year of my contract.

Normally, when a senior officer left the organisation, there was some sort of farewell party on the roof of the building we occupied. For me, there was none. I was paid my unused vacation leave and packed my bags for Barbados. Ollye was also in the process of leaving Georgetown as the airline folded its office there. We could have got married and she follow me back to Barbados, but she wanted to remain close to her father, so we went in different directions. We communicated and saw each other occasionally, but it was never the same again.

Haiti

FORTUNATELY, THERE was to be an election in Haiti, and the OAS was putting together an Election Observation team. They needed someone to head that team. I was recommended. The Canadian in charge of the Human Rights Division may have preferred someone of her own nationality, but I had been the one to work on the details of Haiti's potential entry into CARICOM and I spoke French fluently so I was asked to head the team. When Ollye came to visit me there, she accompanied me on a visit to the interior. She did not participate in the meeting, but the helicopter took her to a beach named Labadi, the same name as that of the largest beach in Accra, Ghana. Many tourists came by ship to that beach, but they were never told that they were in Haiti.

I had been to Haiti a few times in the process of preparing Haitians for entry into CARICOM. The business community there wanted to know on what basis one did trade within CARICOM and at least one session of the negotiation took place there. Living in Haiti for the next few months was a different experience. For one thing, I was now part of what was called the International Community. Every Ambassador involved expected me to report on whatever progress had been made in preparation for the election now imminent. It seemed important now that the military had been removed from power in Haiti that normal civilian Government, to wit, a duly fairly elected Senate and House of Deputies, would be established. The fly in the ointment was the potential candidate for the Presidency, Bertrand Aristide.

Jean-Bertrand Aristide had begun his political life as a poor parish priest. He preached a populist message, which appealed to the poor people of Haiti in general. Many of the people I met in Haiti supported him in his earliest incarnation. They later denied that they had ever supported him. Even his staunchest supporter, the mulatte journalist Jean Dominique, had fallen out with Aristide. Jean Dominique owned a radio station and had supported Aristide, even after Cedras had deposed President Aristide. This led to Jean Dominique fleeing from Haiti to Boston until the return of Aristide.

I met Jean Dominique a few weeks before his death. He was, like Aristide, a great speaker of Kryol, French and English. His English was almost 19th century, but beautiful. He talked about his relationship with Aristide. It had gone cold after he had asked Mr. Aristide about some 8 million dollars given for education, which had disappeared. Aristide in his familiar manner of answering in proverbs said that he was the driver of the truck, but that the driver did not always know what was happening on top of the truck. Shortly afterwards, as Jean Dominique was entering his office compound, a gunman drove by and shot both him and his guard dead. There was some speculation that Jean Dominique was about to do an exposé on a drug trafficker that was a close associate of Aristide. That shooting made what had been a very open Haitian media somewhat more careful.

Aristide had seemed an earnest reformer who would do well for Haiti. Duly elected, he was soon ousted by a military which did not share his published dreams for Haiti. He had to flee the country. He launched his appeal to have the military removed in the USA and in Europe, where I first met him.

Somewhere in the process of regaining power with the help of a US Government, which ensured that the military leader, General Cedras went into exile in Central America, Aristide became someone quite unfamiliar. He married a 'mulatte' Haitian-American lawyer and assumed a very different lifestyle from the former poor parish priest. In the Haitian electoral system, where a President may not serve two consecutive terms and is allowed only to serve two terms, Aristide was very present within Haiti. He lived in a fortress near the airport route, protected by a guard of US security persons. He claimed that the Haitian people had given him his house (worth perhaps some 200 million dollars (over US$22 per Haitian!). One entered through a well-protected gate, the vehicle one travelled in was electronically checked for bombs, and one still had to go over a grid that was certain to rip apart one's tyres if it had not been deliberately turned down. In his anteroom, a magnificent space filled with three photos, one of him with president Clinton, another with the former Venezuelan President Carlos Andres Perez, later convicted for dipping into the public purse and one with President Preval. On the other walls was a collection of paintings by famous Haitian artists that were to die for. These he claimed were given to him by artists who recognised the value of having their works on display in such a prominent place.

While Mr. Aristide was not the President of the day, no one doubted that he would be elected for a second term immediately after the current President, Mr. René Preval. It was generally known, however, that while Mr. Preval sat in the Palace, Bertrand Aristide had a hand in the running of the Elections in more than one sense. Haiti still did not have a Permanent Electoral Council. The body headed by a competent legal magnate had been infiltrated by some of Aristide's people. It meant therefore that whatever came into his office was under the scrutiny of Mr. Aristide's team.

Aristide himself complained that the registration process was not sufficiently advanced to give his supporters a chance to cast their ballots. There was also the complaint that in the case of the Senate where voters had to choose three candidates for each province, some voters would only cast one vote for their special candidate, which was unfair. So voting was postponed to the point where the monies provided for the process were exhausted before the actual elections. The International Community was asked to pitch in. France, normally reluctant, came forward on this occasion and the process of monitoring continued. I should point out that in this Community, the most active members were Canada, the USA and to a lesser extent Spain and France. France, closer to Election Day, provided its own election monitoring team. The USA sent down a team headed by some congressional members, but this, in the nature of the terrain to be covered, was more of a gesture than a serious contribution.

I had the largest and best team I have ever worked with. The one obstacle to efficiency, a Caribbean national that had been there to facilitate our arrangements, had to be removed. After that, it was 'cool runnings' all the way to Election Day. The team came from Jamaica, Argentina, Chile, the UK, and the USA etc. My deputy was a member of the OAS Human Rights Unit. They were sent out to all the provinces except the large island off Haiti, Ile de Gonaive, which was considered dangerous. Russian helicopters provided travel. Indeed, in some areas we had to land in cornfields, since there was no landing pad of the simplest sort. The helicopter also provided us with the opportunity to see up close Henri Christophe's Citadel, perched atop a mountain and built at enormous cost in monies and human life. I visited the members of the team located throughout the country. On one occasion in Cap Haitien, I was presented with the key to the city. On all occasions, I met not only with my team, but also with political leaders, of whom they were plenty.

Haiti's complicated electoral system, unlike ours, works towards total voter participation. Constituencies are created in much the same way, but a candidate has to win a majority (not plurality) of the vote to be elected. If no one candidate gets at least 50% plus 1, a second round of elections is held between the two top candidates to determine who becomes the winning candidate to go to the Chamber of Deputies. This system of voting also applies to the Senate, which is also elected, as well as to the Presidential election. Aristide's party, Lavalas (the avalanche) was doing very well and would almost certainly have won a solid majority of the Senate votes as well as in the Chamber of Deputies. But in the fashion of former Haitian dictators, he wanted to win it all and to choose his own opposition.

Consequently, when the elections were eventually held, and we received the raw vote count from the provinces, it was clear that there needed to be a second vote in somewhat less than half of the Senate seats. It was projected that with a second vote, Lavalas would have won at least a two-thirds majority. However, when the Electoral Council had processed the votes, all sorts of changes had been made in vote totals so that Lavalas could win all the seats on the first vote. I wrote a carefully worded letter to the President of the Electoral Council and to President Preval, indicating what had happened. I went in to see the head of the Electoral Council and he indicated that in such a circumstance, he would be unable to sign off on the results.

President Preval called me in to the Palace. He feared that this news would cause some difficulties. I assured him that if Mr. Aristide were prepared to bite the bullet and accept the genuine results, I would be the first to try to bring investment into Haiti. He addressed me as 'Orlando' and seemed hopeful and grateful that I had handled the matter so discreetly. I had, in fact, been giving interviews to the Press on all sorts of issues, but was careful to ensure that this letter went only to the two places it was intended for. What seemed to have happened was that it was leaked to the Press by one of Aristide's people on the Electoral Council. When quoted word for word what the letter said, I could not even deny that such a letter had been written. The cat was out of the bag.

I was naturally blamed for leaking the information to the Press. Interestingly, I had even ensured that only my staff from the field knew about the letter. Graffiti saying things like "A bas Marville" started emerging on walls downtown. We persevered. The count came out in favour of Aristide's rigged results even for the mayorie of Pétionville, a middle–upper middle class suburb of Port-au-Prince.

I had observed the election at a Pétionville voting station. The turnout was incredible. The crowd waiting to vote had stretched around the town square well before voting started. There was the usual push and shove without any real violence. A very pregnant woman appeared and the crowd parted to let her in to vote. When she had voted it parted again to let her out. There was no sign of malfeasance. However, when the raw vote did not favour Aristide's candidate, the voting numbers were changed for him to win!

There was one stumbling block. The Head of the Electoral Council understood what I had shown him and he refused to sign off on the 'new' results. He knew his life was in danger. I had been on very good terms with the US Embassy and even had access to a White House source for statistical information. The gentleman turned to the US Embassy to get him out of the country. The Chargé turned to me. I in turned asked one of my diplomatic colleagues, being certain to speak in German, which I did not believe would have been monitored. A member of my team sat in on the conversation and asked if I was going to speak German all the way through. I nodded. The diplomat at the other end hesitated, but realised there was no other way, and agreed to ferry the gentleman to safety. And so the Head of the Electoral Council was driven across the Dominican Republic border and flown to Boston to join his son.

Aristide put out the disinformation that he had been kidnapped. This would have been sufficient for his fanatic followers to accept. Aristide chose a new Head and his results were ratified. It was now clear that it was not exactly safe for me to remain in Haiti and there seemed little point in waiting for the election of the President. I so informed the OAS and left quietly, leaving my deputy to close the office. CARICOM, although informed of the nature of the results, decided that it would be fine to recognise Haiti as a new member of CARICOM even if the election of the Senate was in no way free and fair. I believe that it was a matter of sentimentality that held Haiti to a lesser standard than they had agreed. I too was sentimental about Haiti. It had been responsible in large measure for the freeing of my ancestors. It had been victimised by the French and ostracised even by the Latins whose Liberator the Haitians had entertained and trained. But we should not now have held them to any lesser standard to satisfy a man who had now become a power hungry villain. My last efforts were to give a report to the OAS in Washington DC, and to the OAS General Assembly at a meeting on Canouan, St. Vincent.

Barbados Once More

I RETURNED to Barbados, technically retired, but wanting to work at something. I had met an old friend in Washington DC who introduced me to a company that built houses of a material that was cooler than the cement block structures that we seem to adore.

So, after one brief visit on behalf of the CARICOM Secretariat to Ghana, I decided to go into house building. It was interesting to be in Ghana after all these years. The only part of Accra that was recognisable was downtown. The city had grown from about 250,000 to 2 million. Accra now covered all the space between the old city and the University and between the city centre and Tema, the old port township, initially some 21 miles away. But it was great meeting some of my old friends at the University again. Momouni, the brother of Salifu Dakubu was there as well as the poet who had imitated Yevtushenko's style so well. To cap it off, Wen Su-Tung came up to the University from the Ministry of Agriculture. He looked almost as young as he did over three decades before. Yet it did not seem the same. One cannot really go home again.

Before I had gone back to Barbados, I had had at a CARICOM Heads of Government Meeting a brief chat with the Barbados Prime Minister, Owen Arthur. He suggested that I come see him whenever I returned to Barbados. He wanted to make use of what he called my talents. I tried to do so, but evidently Billie Miller, whom I had 'offended' by going to CARICOM, may have told him something to the effect that he could hire me over her dead body. Nothing came from my effort. So nothing came of that offer.

I had been in Barbados quite often both during my time at CARICOM and even before while I was posted to the USA and to several European countries. So it was not that difficult feeling at home here. There was one serious problem. Ollye had persuaded me to buy some land near the beach. An unscrupulous Sindhi, Kiko Chatrani, sold me a bit of land which he did not own. I had been careful to have him give me a cheque in the event that something went wrong. He issued the cheque, which naturally bounced. I later won a case in court against him, but he seemed to have put all his property in someone else's name and nothing could be garnished. I however managed to locate a bailiff, who over a long period, managed to get me back the basic sum.

I desperately needed something to do. I got a job writing a column for the *Nation* newspaper. That provided a little money, but did not in any way feel as if I was at work. I began with a funny article about rum shop talk, but concentrated more on Africa. In the meantime, I took up the challenge of building houses with the new material. My first error was to have a technical person who was as exaggerated in his plans as he was obese. The money put into the effort was mine. The second and perhaps even more serious error was to have a project manager who was a drunk.

We nonetheless managed to build the house on a spot owned by someone I had encountered from the distant past. He became very upset when we rented out the house. My fourth partner managed to talk to him and some sort of arrangement was agreed to. In the meantime, I tried to contact the Minister of Housing, who was the elected representative of the constituency where I lived. I needed him to look at the house and possibly recommend it to his Ministry. It was cheaper, cooler and sturdy. The Minister turned up at my apartment for the first time much later, in fact, three weeks before the elections. He drank my rum and promised that he would visit the house I had built. The visit never materialised.

My next two efforts were even greater disasters. My cousin's daughter asked me to build a house of three bedrooms for her. It was family, so I agreed to build it at cost price. It would be a genuine show house and at $98,000 my costs would be covered. I did not include the vagaries of my drunken building manager. I had a second builder who was an extremely talented Guyanese, named Leo. Leo had to return to Guyana for some family business, so the building manager was left on his own and the cost of everything escalated. I was prepared to take the loss that was likely to be incurred, but my cousin, with the exterior of the house completed and very little to be done on the inside, stopped making payments at about $49,000. I could have taken her to court, but it was family.

I lost several thousand dollars on the third and final project. The building manager would sometimes turn up late and even take the workers to a nearby rum shop rather than getting on with the building. The result was that the owner of the building called a halt to the process at a point where Leo had returned and it was going well. He wanted to sue me for failing to keep to the agreed deadline. Nothing came of the case, since he had received in work considerably more than he had contracted for. I was, however, now with little money left to live on.

Two strange things happened at the same time. Dr. Frank Alleyne called me up to the University at Cave Hill and asked me to co-ordinate a foundation course at the University. He was apologetic that he had asked me so late, but I was eager to begin and earn some money.

I also decided that I would use my Guyana experience to further business in Barbados. While in the CARICOM Secretariat, I realised that many items one could get in Barbados were unavailable in Georgetown. I therefore arranged for a meeting with BS&T to discuss two business proposals. The first had little to do with me: it was to propose that they establish a company that made CDs instead of the old plastic records that they still made at WHIRL. The manager at WHIRL also joined me. I proposed that BS&T could in a joint venture produce these discs, which could then be sold duty free throughout CARICOM. Their first reaction was that they did not want any joint venture with Government. I explained that I was not talking about Government; I thought they could team up with some other business entity in the Region. The cost, it was estimated, would be about BDS$5 million. This they considered too much, a rather strange remark since they were known at least at one time to have some $36 million on a savings account, according to popular rumour.

The second proposal was one where I thought I could be directly involved. It was to target the duty free CARICOM market, where senior members of that staff could not get certain foods that were easily available in Barbados. The idea was also to set up a facility that would make it possible for them to obtain their duty free cars from BS&T. I was informed that they already had someone who was responsible for car sales and that they were prepared to sell me cheaply a large freezer so that I could tap into the food element of that market. BS&T's reluctance has since resulted in that company being taken over by Massey of Trinidad and Tobago.

The second really strange thing, which happened to me, was that I received a phone call from Anita Hansson. I had met Anita some thirty plus years before in Freetown and had seen her maybe two years later in Stockholm. I had thought of her the week before, and so when she called and said: "This is Anita," I immediately replied that I knew who it was. We arranged to meet. The rest is a history that I will recall in more detail. I should point out that her call came just before everything had fallen apart.

Anyway, here I was back home after serving abroad, concerning myself with issues like the promotion of Barbadians and other Third World personnel at the UN, chasing after duty free entry of rum into the US market. I had no house of my own other than the one in Oxnard's, which I had promised to sell to my friend Mohamed. I had two parcels of land left. I was eventually forced to sell one lot to pay off the debt that a combination of the slack performance of my building manager and a cousin's refusal to pay half of the monies owed me for the construction of a house for her. The process left me in terrible financial state.

My mother's house in Brittons Hill had been rented to a series of people who had worked with me; so I rented an apartment in St George. I was to live there for quite a few years before returning to my mother's property in Brittons Hill. Somewhere along the line of this uncertainty, as I mentioned before, I picked up a job as a writer of a column for the *Nation* newspaper. I was also called up to the Social Studies Faculty of the University and asked to coordinate a course in Governance. These allowed me to live, since all I had coming in was my pension, which because I had taken a lump sum to buy land, was relatively small and I was not yet eligible for a National Insurance pension.

I was living in St. George in a rented apartment. Anita and I went to Pebbles' Beach early on mornings, I also played bridge with a group of friends, which included Oliver Jackman, my cousins the Chases et al. Life was not going anywhere. My relationship with Ollye was now all but moribund. She did not wish to live far away from her father and there was nothing I could do in Suriname. It was therefore a simple matter of time before the relationship actually died.

Anita became both the time and reason for the end of that relationship. Anita set up as an acupuncturist and plied her craft first in Wildey and then at the house of my old friend, Austin Ward. We got married at the house of a dear friend Nkosi McIntosh. His young daughter Tetta was the flower girl. In attendance were my mother, Annika, a close friend of Anita's and a handful of the friends we had made. I remember Cardinal Warde, Oliver Jackman and his wife Annie, Peter and Pam Laurie and Dorothy Tatum, who ensured that Anita arrived later than everybody else. It was not the lavish Church wedding that Bajans seem to adore, but an Anglican priest for whom Anita and I have a lot of time, Father Hatch, conducted it. We now continued to live in the apartment I rented in Valley View. We later went on our honeymoon, thanks to the generosity of our friend Cardinal Warde, to Warde's time-share in Cancun, Mexico.

I had met Anita first in Sierra Leone where her husband and I were both working for the UN system, he in ILO and I in UNESCO. I thought she was one of the most beautiful women I had ever seen. So we had both a public and private relationship. I also saw her when I went to Sweden to have an operation done on a knee I had injured playing basketball in Ghana. I had met orthopaedic surgeons who could have done the operation, but they did not have the facilities in West Africa. After that Anita and I had not seen or heard each other for thirty years. Then there was the telephone call. She had evidently not initially intended to come to Barbados. It was, however, the right call at the precise time as our subsequent life has shown.

Her first husband had died when they had gone on a birthday vacation to Bali. Interestingly, my wife Adé had divorced me about the same time. Anita and I did not communicate at that time, but when once she arrived in Barbados and telephoned me, I knew exactly who it was on the other end of the line.

My life stabilised soon after we had met once again. The two part time jobs provided the wherewithal to live and my own life seemed to move into a different sphere. Then, I received a call from the Governor-General, Sir Clifford Husbands, to ask me to serve as an independent member of the Senate. My mother and Anita attended the swearing in ceremony. Then, nearly every Wednesday I had to attend meetings of the Senate. I wrote about corruption as a result of one of the meetings of a Senate sub-committee and was duly fired by the *Nation* newspaper, for which I had been writing a weekly column. I however served for several years in the Senate, discussing issues that ranged from education to foreign affairs. My maiden speech, however, was on a proposed law, which had some glaring human rights issues. I naturally objected to the law.

During the BLP Government of that period, I had had a

number of reasons for intervening in the Senate. One was the inordinate amount of money spent on remodelling Kensington Oval, which one famous cricketer felt was one of the three historic grounds in the world, after only Lords and the Gabba. My objection was not specifically to the destruction of a historic cricket oval, but to the inordinate cost of rebuilding it. With the purchase of the land involved, the removal of the inhabitants of the area and the purchase of an alternative site and housing to resettle them, even before one got to the rebuilding of the stands and expansion of the grounds, the inclusion of a water area and all the other trappings, the cost was said to be somewhere in the region of BDS$400 million. What was even worse was that no lights had been installed and the final match was decided by the absence of light toward the end of the game!

I had made two points. An expenditure of such sums was not justified unless one could make the monies back in ten years and there seemed little prospect of that. Additionally, it was silly to continue building everything of value in the city area. It would have been better to transform the grounds of an already existing oval in St. Philip, where an additional five acres (2 hectares) were being offered as a gift to Government for that purpose. What is more, cricket would have the advantage that when everyone was going into the city for work, those going to the game would be travelling in the opposite direction. The same would be true after the game. However, it was clear that the stakes involved in transforming Kensington were high and the voice of reason counted for little. My intervention did nothing to avert the financial disaster that followed. Indeed, the Ministry of Tourism hiring a ship to house visitors to the game compounded that. These were expected to be from a part of the cricketing world that was eliminated before the final round. So the ship was an additional unnecessary cost.

One of my final contributions in the Senate was when a UN Bill was used instead of the more stringent bill the Integrity Commission which I had chaired had proposed. The UN Bill had passed the house easily and in the Senate, the process was much the same, with speaker after speaker saying that Barbados was 15th on the list of least corrupt countries and better than the USA or UK. When I spoke, I pointed out that both the USA and UK had Freedom of Information laws, which made it more difficult to hide corruption, while we had no such law in spite of the work the Integrity Commission had done on preparing such a draft bill, and that in any case, if we were the fifteenth least corrupt country, we were corrupt! Interestingly, only one other Senator, Dr. Ester Byer repeated my assertion that we were corrupt and that we should be worried about that.

Just before the incoming Governor-General removed me from the Senate, I was asked by the Minister of Foreign Affairs to lead the Barbados delegation to Geneva for Barbados' Human Rights annual report. A very efficient Foreign Service Officer and the 'Ombudsman', who played virtually no role in the proceedings, accompanied me. In the Barbados Mission in Geneva, the Ambassador and her staff pitched in on the drafting of the speech I was to deliver. We knew that the likely criticism was that we still had the mandatory death sentence on the books (now removed) and sodomy was criminalised, even though we did not prosecute anyone for homosexual activity unless it was rape, with a minor, or in public. We therefore explained that with the burden of general legislation, we tended to omit certain segments even if we made sure that no one fell victim in these two areas. We had, for instance, not executed anyone for 34 years. The presentation went well. Geneva was still a cold and very expensive place.

After Sir Clifford became the first native Governor-General to resign and not die in office, his successor thought he would stamp his own mark on the Senate and replaced me and three other Senators, including two brilliant women, with four men.

Interestingly, back at the University, my position changed when a full-time lecturer was put in charge of the course. She promptly fired me and hired one of her cronies. This lasted for a year until she managed to irritate management so totally that I was asked to return to lead the course. I was able to bring on Clyde Griffith, whom I had taught at the Modern High School several decades before and who had had a long political career in the Barbados Labour Party. We continued to work together along with a third lecturer for several years since then. The third lecturer managed to arrange her own demise by becoming involved in a case of plagiarism.

During the year away from the University, I wrote a novel that had been somewhere in the back of my head for somewhat more than a decade. It was about Sierra Leone, although not historically or geographically accurately so, and a mythical Caribbean island called Fonseca. The title of the novel was *Children of the Shadows*. I was in my early seventies when I completed my first novel. Even Henry Miller, who was also a late starter, had written his first novel in his early sixties. It was launched at the Law School of the University of the West Indies, thanks to the effort of my 'junior brother', Professor Albert Fiadjoe with whom I had studied at the University of Ghana. (Many of the Ghanaians of that era had become outstanding figures either in law or economics. Even the President of Ghana and the leader of the Opposition had been at the University of Ghana at the same time as I had).

A compendium of the fairy tales we were told as children (plus a few others) retold in a completely different fashion, followed that novel. It was in fact a parody of these stories. It was called *The Prissy Princess and Other Adult Fairy Tales*. It was not adult in the sense of an adult movie, though segments of it would be rated TV14. Albert was no longer in Barbados and this book was launched in Hastings. It earned one rave review, but not many Bajans seem to read beyond newspapers, so sales were not spectacular. A local publisher put out both books. She ran into financial difficulties and had, at first, been less than forthcoming in terms of my payments or some promised copies of the first book. That relationship has subsequently improved with the management of sales and receipts coming directly to me from Amazon et al.

Brittons Hill

THE BRITTONS Hill property became badly neglected by a series of tenants including a St. Lucian calypsonian who refused to pay back rent and suggested I take him to court. I did and won. However, the bailiffs sent to deliver the judgement and exact payment said they could not find him! The monies owed have grown, but he seems no longer to be here in Barbados. Subsequent tenants were not great housekeepers. I gave them a simple tree to plant in front of the house, but they let the tree die. So we decided to freshen up the place and move in.

The property now has some fifteen or so fruit trees in the backyard and three towering trees in front of the house. This has made the house cooler and has provided a canopy under which I can park my car. We also had to acquire two dogs, since some person or persons had the habit of entering the front yard and stealing whatever they could from the porch. This has since stopped.

The two dogs were a story in themselves. Zho, the smaller one, sneaked out under the backyard fence one evening and we went all over the neighbourhood looking for the pesky little thing. After a long time searching—

darkness had fallen—we returned and there he was. He had evidently only wanted to explore the outside world, but there was no food or other interesting discovery forthcoming there, so he returned. Some children loved the dogs and others were afraid of them. Two very well dressed and well-behaved Rastafarian children would come and ask if they could see the dogs. Others would cower as they passed by the house. In fact even grown-ups were scared of them, even though as dogs go, they were rather gentle.

Anita became the front and centre of my life. I had lived so long alone that it was all the more pleasurable to have her constant company. At first there were some awkward moments, since she did not feel that she could be left alone at receptions for more than ten seconds, but she gradually found her feet in the society and became more self-assured. We have travelled to various Caribbean islands on vacation as well as to Stockholm to visit her children and to Washington DC and Maryland to see mine and to visit with my mother who lived there. Mom, who lived in the USA, would also come to Brittons Hill for stints during the cold Maryland winter months.

Anita became so much a part of the family that even my ex-wife liked her and she has been a big hit with my grandchildren. One little one said to her: "I have three grandmothers and they are all beautiful." That is high praise for anyone from a child. Anita too is very comfortable in her skin. As she put it, referring to me, "He is black, I am white; he is big and I am small: no difference at all really." On top of that, having lived in Africa for some ten years, having climbed Kilimanjaro three times, an admirer of Julius Nyerere, and having with her late husband adopted a Tanzanian, she has black grandchildren. Indeed all her children and grandchildren consider all of each other and us as family. All the grandchildren call me Opa (German for grandfather) and mine call her Oma. I suggested that moniker even to my own grandchildren for them to distinguish between their other grandfathers and me. Sadly, one of the other ones passed away rather early in their lives.

Settling back in Brittons Hill was interesting. Very few of the people I knew were still there. Mrs. Grant and her rumshop were still there. I of course remembered her and her children and even passed some time there including one occasion when I had lunch with David Thompson. When Mom came down, she also visited with Mrs. Grant, but she loved best of all to go to the beach. She could not swim; even my father had failed to teach her how to swim. But she loved sitting at the water's edge and being wet by the incoming waves.

Then Mom began to change. She would ask the same question over and over. When we went to Maryland, we stopped her driving. She was 92 and not any longer the brilliant driver she had been in her youth. She had even lost some of the flair she had when I was driving. Sometimes, when we visited family in New York and had to return late at night to Maryland, she would ensure that she talked to me all the way back, so that I would not fall asleep. My children would be fast asleep in the back seat. Arrived home, she would fall asleep immediately. On another occasion on a long journey in Europe, she observed that there was another driver who set a pace for me and then would fall back so that I could set the pace.

But that flair had dissipated. I also would read a novel on the plane and then pass it on to her. She enjoyed that. Now, however she only read her Bible. Then finally, she stopped reading altogether. It was difficult to observe this, since she had read at least one book a week when she was younger. It was she who had made me interested in books. Sometimes she forgot to eat, even though she always had tons of food in her apartment. Then it happened. She fell one day and broke her hip. It healed very well, but the experience of being for quite a while in hospital threw her directly into full-blown Alzheimer's.

It was November and I could not easily leave the course I was teaching to go live with her. So Anita went. Her task was to persuade Mom that she should return to Barbados. I am not sure that I could have done that. But Anita succeeded. So I flew up and we came back to Barbados on one of the most horrendous flights I have ever had. I was angry with the stewardess who took no notice of my mother's needs, so I was forced to say some things I would not normally have said. Whoever was in charge of the plane came up to me and said that he had authority on a US plane as we then were. I naturally reminded him that plane had landed in Barbados where there was no other jurisdiction. Embarrassed by my calling his bluff, he called the local policemen who found no reason for arresting me, so my mother, my wife and I were finally allowed to leave the plane.

Arrived finally at Brittons Hill, Mom was more than a handful. She kept us up all night. My cousin Vere offered to take her to church one Sunday and keep her for a day. When he brought her back, it was evident that he had gone through the same ordeal that we had. So I went with Rasta, our handyman, to look at Nursing Homes. The one we liked best was a simple place in Tudor Bridge at the back of Strathclyde. It turned out to be an excellent choice.

All at the place loved Mom. She would make them laugh. Medicated, she was extremely funny and she was always travelling around in her wheel chair. On one occasion, when she was lying on a sofa and I asked her if she wanted to sit up, she said yes. We spoke for about fifteen seconds before I repeated the question and she said no. I reminded her that she had just said yes. "But that was then!" she quipped.

On another occasion, she said she was getting married. Anita who was great at conducting these weird exchanges asked who was the bride. "A young woman," she replied. Anita then opined that young women made excellent spouses and the conversation continued as if it were the most normal exchange between two persons.

Mom only recognised Anita and me. Vere and his wife Betty would visit and she would mistake him for my son Wolé. My daughter Aderonké and her two children also visited on one occasion, with Leila, the smaller one sitting in Mom's lap, but although she loved the idea of a child sitting on her lap, she could not remember who Leila was. Leila was doing what her mother had done decades before, when she would ask Mom "Which is the bad knee?" to be sure that she only sat on the good one. Now she had no good knee.

Oddly, though, Mom said she wanted to have a 95th birthday party. Soon after she said that, she fell very ill and had to be taken to the hospital. I was again not very happy with the treatment she received there. I had to hire nurses throughout the period because the nursing assistants were not allowed to do much in the way of care. She then had bedsores, a phenomenon which had never once occurred at the nursing home. Evidently, they could do nothing with her at the Queen Elizabeth Hospital, so she was returned to the nursing home. Mom had once said that she knew the day she would die. She probably did. She remained semi-conscious from then on until her 95th birthday, where she had said she wanted a special birthday party. On her birthday, she woke up and had very normal telephone conversations with her sister and with my daughter, Aderonké. Then her party followed.

When the party for her 95th birthday ended, she fell back into a state of semi-consciousness and remained in that state until she died a week later. The funeral occurred two weeks later in order to allow relatives from New York and the Washington area to arrive in Barbados. One dear friend of hers, Janet Yerenkye, also came with the cousins from New York, her sister and Aderonké from Maryland. I tried to make it a special funeral. The Prime Minister could not make the funeral, but he visited the funeral home in St. Lucy to see the body before it was interred. The St. Lucy Representative attended and sat prominently up front with the relatives.

As one of my local cousins said, "If one can say a funeral was beautiful, it was the most beautiful funeral I have ever seen." I had invited the Mighty Gabby to sing a song for Mom, so he brought along his guitar and sang the Lord's Prayer. My daughter read a passage from the Bible, my wife, who now says: "She was my mother too," spoke as did Aunt Gwen, Mom's sister. Vere declaimed the lines of some obscure psalm. Vere has a prodigious memory still and therefore did not need to read anything. The Priest, who seemed constantly baffled, looked about to see where the lectern was placed and he seemed even more confounded when Gabby mounted the stage. It was almost as if he feared that Gabby would launch into some unholy calypso.

What was best though was that Aunt Gwen who had been crying and seemed nearly unable to walk, mounted the podium and stood before the microphone and gave a rousing vote of praise for her sister. No one knew exactly how she had mustered that strength. It was brilliant. I also spoke of my version of Mom's life. I repeat the entire eulogy, even though it repeats some of the events I have already chronicled.

"First of all I wish to thank my wife Anita and staff of Elin Fort Nursing Care for the love and devotion they showered on my mother during the last many months of her life.

Today, however, we are not here merely to inter the body of a deceased; we are also here to celebrate the long and generally beautiful life of a mother. I refer to my mother as a mother, largely because she was not only my mother, but also the mother of all my friends who all followed me in calling her Mom. Indeed, even my children called her Mom, except for the last one who insisted on calling her Nana. There was no child that Mom did not automatically love. And her grandchildren knew that well. And they too reciprocated her vast love.

Enid Verona Marville was born not too far to the North East of here and spent much of her early life southwest of here at Gilkes.

She went to school at the Mess House with Dame Nita as her senior and young Errol Barrow, her contemporary going to the boys' school across the yard. She was bright and could have gone on to secondary school and possibly to University, if such opportunities existed in those days for ordinary poor people. One day, she paid a clairvoyant a penny to tell her future. She thought she had misspent her penny and was very angry at herself, as all the clairvoyant could tell her was that she would have a son and that her life would be fuller each year after that. On leaving school, therefore, she was asked to teach at the same school. That ended, however, when I came on to the scene. In those backward days, a woman could not teach if she were pregnant. So Mom was forced to do what had to be done, by becoming a nanny. This did not end too well as Mom had lost none of her great sense of identity and pride in herself. So one day when I was none too well and she stayed at home for an extra hour to look after me, she arrived late to work. As was normal in those days of what I call discreet slavery, the lady of the house berated her and explained that she had had to take care of Master Timothy herself. My mother explained in rather forthright terms that she had had to look after her own child and could not see why it was an imposition for her employer to look after her own for just for an hour. Thereupon she took her belongings and left the job.

Mom continued in this field until she graduated to being a dental helper in Bridgetown. By then I was at school in Bridgetown and both my mother and father had drifted there after jobs. She also had some words with her new employer concerning me, but that employer was not Bajan so it never came to separation. Mom continued to review her options and she took a spell at selling lunch snacks in Tweedside market. She was very popular there because as usual she was her friendly self, full of advice. One indication of this was one day, when I came home from abroad; a taxi driver stopped and told me to get in. He was driving a brand new taxi and he was insistent. He informed me that it would cost me nothing wherever I wanted to go. My mother was responsible for the car, he explained. Evidently, he had gone to consult her about what he should buy. He brought a nice looking car with him. My mother advised that it looked good, but that he might find out that the engine was not as good as the exterior. He went back with a cheap beat-up old car and she said: "Patch it up and it will work for you." He did as instructed, and he said he had made enough money from that old car to be able to buy this brand new one. He had been one of the lunch clients at my mother's market stall.

She continued her move upward and was asked to run a guest-house. The owner had promised her concrete blocks whenever she was ready to build her new house. Hurricane Janet had affected us and Mom wanted to build in stone. She was married to Douglas Garvey, now adding to her already long name. He was a chef on a ship and was at home perhaps less than half of the year. This did not worry Mom who was by nature independent anyway. When she was ready to build, the blocks were not forthcoming, so she asked if I could lend her some money and she would pay me back.

Mom took off for the USA and had paid every cent back in a year. She continued there and paid all the necessary bills for the house until my stepfather died. I took over responsibility for the house after that. She became settled in Long Island, New York where she took care of the mother of one of the stars of *Days of Our Lives*. Such people are not overly generous, so she did not become comfortable off this job. She however managed to help an old lady with Parkinson's to survive for ten years. The son gave her a parting bonus of $1000!

Mom then decided that she would formalize her work experience by doing a course in Nursing. I had by now been posted to Washington, DC and the house provided was ample, so I suggested that she could do the course in Washington and live with my wife and our two children. She finished her nurse's aide course with all A's and thought of continuing to the full nursing qualification, but opted for a job at a geriatric hospital within walking distance from our home. She also opted for the early shift so that she could pickup my two daughters after school. This relationship continued till after my son was born and was allowed to sneak out of his room each night and end up in my mother's. We were aware of this unofficial arrangement and each night we would go and retrieve him while he was fast asleep.

Later when I was posted to Brussels, my mother moved into her own flat and added to her work at the hospital by learning and doing pottery as well as crochet. She travelled all into Western Maryland to buy yarn to make her blankets, hand towels and baby clothes. Typically, she made little money from these exploits since she always talked about not wanting to charge people too much money.

In the summer, she travelled to Brussels with my son—the daughters were now grown up—and we travelled throughout Europe. The first year all three children along with her sister, present here today, came. Mom wanted to go to Sweden since I had studied and lived there. She loved it. This was heightened when we were about to return to Brussels, where the young son of the house where we stayed asked: "But Nana, who is going to cook those great meals for us now?"

That was good. Next time around she wanted to see Venice. So we drove off for Venice. On the way back she wanted to see her namesake, the city of Verona. Next we visited Luxembourg, then Paris on another occasion. She also visited Strasbourg with my son, Wole and me. It was on the occasion of Nelson Mandela's first visit to Europe after his lengthy incarceration. I represented the Caribbean and I took my 6-7 year old son with me. Mr. Mandela shook his hand and said something to him with Wole showing all the poise of a grown boy. When Mr. Mandela returned to the hotel where we also were ensconced, he left the cortege and came over to Wole once more and said: "Good to see you again, young man." My mother turned to Wole afterwards and said: "You may not understand this now, but this will be one of the great moments of your life." Wole said: "Yes, Nana," and then, turning to me, continued: "Dad let's be cool about this. Don't go telling everybody."

I had also travelled to Egypt and to India. Mom wanted to go there too. So on my final year in Brussels, she Wole and I flew to Cairo. We saw the Sphinx and the pyramids at Giza and travelled up the Nile to Luxor, the Valley of the Kings and the magnificent palace of Ramses. I could not go to India with her, so she decided to do it on her own. She would go visit the sister of a friend of ours here in Barbados and then spend a month at an Ayurvedic Hospital in Trivandrum.

Arrived at the airport, she saw no one there to meet her. Evidently her hostess had been informed that the plane would be two hours late. Mom simply went outside, asked if anyone knew where she wanted to go—in India and

Japan there is not even the signposting that we are accustomed to. But Mom arrived safely and returned to Maryland with much better knees than she had left with, Brave, very brave lady she was, and really tough, as someone once said.

Since her passing, my friends have said all sorts of beautiful things about her. She was strong. She was vibrant. She was a powerful personality. "She stands high in my estimation; she was a remarkable woman." She was funny! Indeed she was always as funny as she was brave. Evidently she kept the nurses at the nursing home constantly entertained. For me, her wit was quick and spontaneous. Even with an impaired mind, she was good. On one of the many occasions when we went to visit her, she was lying on a sofa. Anita, my wife asked her if she wanted to get up. She replied in the affirmative. Some brief conversation occurred. It must have been for about fifteen seconds. Then I asked her if she wanted to get up. "No," she said.

"But you just said that you wanted to get up," I continued.

"Yes," said, "But that was then."

The story of my mother would not be complete without my telling about her cricket exploits. Mom was a genuine Tantie Merle. That apart, she knew her game. She used to bowl to me, so that I could learn to bat. Better than that, one day in Mount Standfast, there was a pick up match.

There were however only 21 men, so the brother of a very distinguished gentleman who wanted very much to be sitting here today, said to my mother: "You're always talking 'bout cricket. Why you don't come and play?"

So Mom went in, changed into a pair of trousers and joined a team. When Frank Worrell came out to bat, no one wanted to bowl at him, so they gave the ball to my mother. In her second ball, a gentle off break, my mother clean bowled Frank Worrell! Not only is that a very poignant memory of an incredible woman. I would also wish to end with the question: Is there anyone here whose mother has clean bowled the likes of Sir Frank Worrell?"

Aunt Gwen became nearly inconsolable once again when they interred the body. Anita and I still talk about Mom ever so often. It would be difficult to forget someone so formidable a human being.

Brittons Hill was a significant place in my life. I had left Barbados for England from my mother's house in Brittons Hill. We were now back there. That small wooden house, that I had left nearly a half-century before, had been transformed into a not so small wall house. Returning to it after my stepfather had expired and various people had rented it and left it relatively dilapidated, Anita and I set about making it more liveable. My mother had in 1971 built a house that had comfortable rooms and we did not have much to do there. We added to the two bedrooms at the back of the house, so that we could put in a semi-bath in the event that anyone else visited. We also set about planting trees. We had prepared a flamboyant and a sweet tamarind from a box of sweet tamarinds we had been given one Christmas. We planted the flamboyant along with a neem out front. We also planted two neems, one in the middle backyard and the other on the outside backyard. Eventually we planted a Jamaican ackee out front and had to cut down the flamboyant since it was crushing the ackee and running into the electricity and telephone lines.

Anita busied herself with planting ferns and something she calls a ceramic plant and generally working on things in the outer yard. At first, local villagers would pass by and simply look at this strange European woman out in the sun, not knowing that she had lived in Africa, taught a group of Tanzanian women to sew clothes as a means of making their own money or that she was as comfortable with these women as she was on top of Kilimanjaro. Eventually, they realised that she was a permanent feature of the landscape and would say good morning or good evening or good night at any hour after midday. Nowadays, everyone who passes greets her and she behaves as if she is part of the village.

Anita is a beautiful person. In the beginning she had severe problems at night, since the death of her former husband haunted her. That too passed and she began saying that Arne, her deceased husband and I were very much alike. I do not quite understand that, since Arne was a very gentle man and I make no pretensions to being one. Evidently, he was also funny. I have never felt so comfortable with anyone. During the writing of my first book, she had no difficulty with my getting up in the middle of the night and writing in those hours, which are so beautifully quiet and productive.

One day, I ran into a Rastafarian whom everybody called Rasta. He was trimming grass with a weed whacker. I asked him how much he charged and, since his fees were very reasonable, I hired him. Rasta lived in the house of someone who had let him house sit for the family. When they returned, he was forced to sleep in an old car. When we discovered this, we converted an old building I had put up in the yard from left over materials from my building days so that he had a bedroom there. It was a leap of faith in someone whom we hardly knew, but he has been totally honest and a boon to the household. Rasta has turned out to be an incredible asset. He has become a sort of handyman, since he can fix most things. He is a vegetarian like Anita and therefore his diet does not become a problem. We bought him a suitable bed and provided him with a radio, a table and chairs. His baptised name is Randolph Jones, but even my grandchildren call him Uncle Rasta.

Rasta knows everybody in the area. There may be those he does not directly know, but he invariably knows someone who knows that person intimately. He therefore can throw up a needed plumber or electrician at a moment's notice. We consider the salary we pay him, the lodging and the three meals a day we provide as being the best expenditure we incur each month. He too is grateful that he has a permanent home and he loves dogs. Well after Zho died from accidental poisoning, we acquired another rather big dog, BoBo. Rasta constantly talks to him to ensure that he is well behaved, an almost impossible task for a pup that loves raw vegetables and cheese and is on top of that probably the most intelligent dog we have ever had. If we bring home shopping in a cardboard box, he waits until we have unpacked the contents of the box, takes the box out into the yard and tears it into small pieces, which Rasta can dispose of more easily.

Brittons Hill has become our genuine home. Mom spent several uncomfortable weeks here before we put her in a nursing home. Interestingly, I took Rasta with me to look at various homes and ended up with the smallest and cosiest one, the Elin Forte nursing home. When we came back and reported our find to Anita, she merely said that she was sure we had made the best choice. It also turned out to be. Mom was always humorous and the staff appreciated this and treated her specially. It seems only proper therefore that we should treat this house as near sacred. I do not propose to sell it and I need to say in my will that it can be improved by building another storey to it, but that it remain a Marville homestead.

Returning to the topic of my wife, she is not an angel.

Like many a woman I have known, she can get angry and go off on a tangent. In Anita's case, this involves waiting until bedtime to bring up some complaint. As she once put it, it is necessary to complain. I am not sure what that means, but I know she very occasionally puts the principle into practice. That invariably means a long unpleasant session. Yet the following morning she is once again the beautiful person I love.

When she is beautiful, she is unsurpassable. We spend a few hours a week at the beach. Brown's Beach is our beach. We never go anywhere else. Initially (when we lived in St. George) we went early in the morning to Pebbles beach, but the water there is considerably more turbulent. Brown's beach is the best beach I have ever visited. The water is usually clear and one can see that clear water as far out as the fishing boats. Initially we used to swim out to the boats, but one day, Anita was stung by a Portuguese man-of-war and had to be taken to the doctor for an anti-histamine shot. Since that day we have swum sideways down to the blue boats further along the bay. It is about two hundred metres. I sometimes walk back. Anita is a great swimmer. She never walks and will occasionally swim over to the Marine Reserve and back after our routine sea trek.

And we write. I am often busy at writing articles for the *Advocate* newspaper or writing something creative. She is writing a sort of memoir called *Letters to Gilda*, which should turn out to be quite a book. She is writing in English, because she insists that Swedish is such a small language. One of her past relatives, a famous Swedish poet, Stig Dagerman, would probably disown her from his grave. She now reserves Swedish for talking to me in bed, when she is tired. Occasionally, she asks me what the translation for a particular Swedish word is into English. My Swedish has therefore had some solid practice. It was the first new language I learnt after French. It is not a very useful language outside Sweden, but it helps in words in German and Dutch as well as its sister language, Norwegian.

Back in 2007, I joined Brandford Taitt in what were numerous Saturday morning sessions as a sort of Assistant Coach for the DLP candidates vying for electoral office. Just about this time, we became rather close friends of the Chinese Ambassador and his wife. He had good reason for this. I too had been an Ambassador and understood his concerns. One concern arose from propaganda put out by the BLP that the DLP, if they won the coming elections would revert to recognising Taiwan as China, an error that we were unlikely ever to commit. He needed to assure Beijing that this was not going to happen. I informed him that the entire scenario had been cooked up and that I had contact with the new political directorate.

Thus, almost immediately after the elections, my wife and I were invited to visit China. That was easy since I was a member of the Senate and it did not breach any protocol. We visited Beijing, Shanghai and Xian. We were accompanied wherever we went by a rather officious protocol officer who behaved more like a chaperone. In Beijing, my wife visited her old acupuncture professor and bought herself some needles and other materials. We visited various sites, but did not go to the Great Wall as my knee was in bad shape.

Shanghai was a fabulous experience. We travelled up river and back, ate at an old beautiful restaurant as well as one of the more fashionable ones on the riverbank. Tall skyscrapers lined the river and it was clear that we were in one of the new great world cities, an ancient city that had morphed into something completely modern and beautiful. It was also a cleaner version of cities like New York or London. One could not but be impressed.

From Shanghai we flew to Xian, the site of the fabled terra cotta statues. An old Emperor had had a complete army carved in life-like terra cotta with their horses, chariots etc. What was interesting was that every soldier was unique. Some were taller than others, and all had different faces. It was as if each soldier had been an exact representation of an individual soldier. We were privileged to see what was, to our minds, one of the wonders of the ancient world. The only thing that spoiled the visit was when I wanted to buy a souvenir from one of the unauthorised sellers of terra cotta representations. The chaperone strenuously objected. Being me, I proceeded to buy one. We then flew back to Shanghai and New York.

Back in Barbados, I even wrote vignettes for 28 of the

30 candidates for the various campaigns. At the end of the election, which the DLP won handsomely, Taitt was offered the Presidency of the Senate and he pleaded to have me made Vice President, but no political spoils fell my way. I was instead asked to chair an Integrity Commission that was to have drafted laws covering the Integrity of parliamentarians, produce a Freedom of Information Bill along with an Ombudsman Bill, A Contractor General Bill, a new Defamation Bill and a Bill limiting the number of Governments a Prime Minister could run to two. It was agreed that Dr. Albert Fiadjoe (my junior brother as he calls himself and a brilliant legal mind) would draft the pieces of legislation involved; the Commission would review the Drafts and take them to the public for any input they would make.

We achieved this with the Freedom of Information Draft Bill and the public made some useful additions to the draft. It was presented to the CPC after I had had a session with the Permanent Secretaries and the Cabinet. The PS's were the first persons we had invited to review the Bill. They only responded when they realised that the Bill would move forward. One even suggested that any monies spent on staffing freedom of information could be better spent on increasing their staff quotas. The other bits of proposed legislation fared even worse fates. Two PS's objected to the Contractor General Draft on the grounds that they were in the process of revising the public tender systems. Several years later, the draft is still in limbo. One Minister objected to the Defamation draft. He was a lawyer. The Integrity Bill was left aside in favour of a gentler UN anti-corruption Bill which was passed into law without the conduct of Ministers clause, which was to have been drafted by the Ministers themselves and the Ombudsman draft has equally gone nowhere, since the old ombudsman was reappointed. The Commission has, in the meantime, expired.

It later occurred to me that I had been given a dead end assignment, possibly because David Thompson did not want me anywhere near the political directorate, when once they had won the election. Even after David Thompson had died, I was constantly promised by his successor that he would come by my house to have a chat with me. That has naturally not yet materialised. On the eve of my leaving the Senate, I was awarded the CBE on the Queen's birthday in 2013.

When I look back, I realised that one of the reasons why I joined in the DLP fight to overthrow the BLP regime was that corruption had become all too familiar not only among politicians but also among the private sector they dealt with. I am not at all sure that that has changed. I still view corruption as the single most important factor in poverty in a developing country and one of the most potent forces against the development of that country. While we normally look to Nigeria for an example of widespread corruption, we do have a great deal of corruption in our Caribbean countries and that is where we should focus our attention. Corruption puts a brake on development, as individuals seek fortunes rather than what is good for the society as a whole.

Travels, Mainly in Africa

LOOKING BACK, I had travelled pretty much throughout the world either before I was employed as a diplomat or afterwards. In Australasia, I have been in Fiji, Papua New Guinea, New Zealand and Australia. In Asia, I have been in India, China and Japan. I made one brief and uncomfortable stop in Saudi Arabia and spent a few days in Singapore. In Europe, I have been in all the countries of Western Europe (except Finland), as well as in the Czech Republic and in Slovakia and in all the countries, which at one time comprised Yugoslavia.

In Africa, I had covered all of the countries with a coast, except the Lusophone countries and several of those in the spine of the continent, like Tunisia and Libya, Niger, Sudan, South Sudan, the Central African Republic, Rwanda and Burundi, The Democratic Republic of Congo, Botswana and Lesotho. I was in only one of the island states of Africa, Mauritius. I also did not visit Namibia.

As I indicated before, Ghana, my first country in Africa—West Africa to be precise—had a profound impact on me. I have never felt more at home anywhere outside the Caribbean than in Ghana. There were too aspects of that country that I have not covered. I made a trip once to Wa, in the northwest, which continued to Tamale in the North. That was an experience in itself. When one is accustomed to the greenery of the South, the road to the North is barren of foliage except for the odd baobab tree. The roads were all yellow-brown laterite and when not wet by rain, extremely dusty. I believe that that has all changed since my last visit to Ghana.

In Ghana, I played a lot of cricket and played on the national team against Nigeria where I made 1, 42 and 50 not out in a fifty over match. I also had a five-wicket haul. But there were considerably better cricketers in Ghana than in Sierra Leone where I was recognised as a cricketer.

I remember returning to Sierra Leone once close to the six pm deadline for the border closing. One of the young immigration officers spotted me in the line and said: "That's Marville, the cricketer. Let him through!" I am not much for such favouritism, but having possibly to look for somewhere to sleep in that part of Liberia did not appeal to me.

The border between Sierra Leone and Liberia in the North as distinct from this southern crossing was a different matter. There had been a road, but at the time I crossed in a vehicle, one of my passengers had to get out of the vehicle and direct me as if I were going on to a ramp in a repair shop. The holes between such ridges were enormous: we could not afford to fall into one of them. We covered six miles in about three hours before we were back onto one of the laterite 'pistes' so familiar in West

Africa.

In southern Africa by contrast, there were beautifully made tarred roads that allowed for inordinate speeds. Interestingly too, while the four Anglophone countries of West Africa have followed their more numerous Francophone neighbours in moving from the traditional British left side of the road to the Napoleonic right, in Southern Africa from Malawi to South Africa and from Swaziland to Namibia, they continued to drive on the left hand side of the road. While the changeover in a highly organised Sweden had had its problems, in West Africa, it all went so smoothly that in Sierra Leone one commentator said that they should change sides every six weeks or so. In Nigeria, the first recorded accident resulting from the change was by a Dutchman who failed to recognise the change back to what he had grown up with and went the wrong way around a roundabout.

On my first visit to South Africa, I did not know whether the South Africans now recognised passports from other Commonwealth countries without a visa, but I was pretty sure they would. I arrived in Johannesburg with a diplomatic passport and presented it to the officer. He did not yet know what to do, so he had someone call Foreign Affairs in Pretoria and they said it was all right. Nelson Mandela was now President and I knew that there would be no difficulty. I had, of course, never visited that country during apartheid and I had similarly avoided the Portuguese colonies of that period. South Africa had become very accommodating to people who looked like me and came from abroad.

In the horn of Africa, I visited Djibouti and Ethiopia (twice). On my first visit to Ethiopia, it was during a period of military rule. I so much wanted to visit Axum, but that was on the battle lines with what later became Eritrea. And there was a curfew. The hotel at which I stayed and at which the meeting was held, put on a party each night and anyone from outside the institution was forced to stay overnight.

I did not get to travel in Ethiopia, which was a pity, since that country was part of the cradle of humanity. I was forced to look out from the hotel on the drab streets of Addis. At that time, whenever there were poor rains, there was a famine in the country. Now things have improved and famine is relegated to its neighbour, Somalia, embroiled in a fight against the jihadist Al Shabab. Ethiopia has improved its harvesting of water and has in fact leased an area of its land in the West of the country to a European food farming enterprise. At that time, Ethiopia's shining glory was its airline, allowed to operate independently. It was easily one of the two or three best airlines I have flown on.

I had no concerns about travel in Djibouti, where a French force posted on the outskirts of the city ensured that the turmoil of Somalia and Ethiopia-Eritrea could not occur. We travelled to the outer edges of the country, the borders with Ethiopia and Somalia. The trip was through vast expanses of desert. There was not even a baobab, the provider of water and sustenance for the traveller in its leaves, fruit and even its bark. There were, however, the odd rib cages of cattle that must have died of thirst in times of absolute drought. It reminded one of the deserts in old cowboy films.

The French kept military forces in their former colonies, normally with the acquiescence of the local leaders. They also cooperated with such leaders whenever it was necessary. For instance, while I was in Cote d'Ivoire, there was an uprising in Man in the north of the country. It was brutally suppressed. It was said that an entire village had been wiped out. No mention was made of this in either Ivoirien or French newspapers. However, absurdly, several months later, the President, Houphet Boigny, was shown shaking the hand of some leader from Man and the photo was titled: *A Reconciliation of Brothers*.

Bouaké in Cote d'Ivoire was my least privileged sojourn in Africa. In every case except Ghana, I had been either a UNESCO expert or a Barbados diplomat or a CARICOM Assistant Secretary General. In Bouaké I was merely a poor village headmaster. We had sold my car in Sierra Leone and therefore all travel was by what is called mammy lorries (ZRs). Such vehicles to Abidjan were rather sophisticated. They were Peugeot vans that seated eight and a driver. However, if one travelled north, it was by mammy lorry.

But travels outside of the tarred road between Bouaké and Abidjan were in less comfortable mammy lorries. I made one trip to Ghana with Mark, the young African American student. He slept very well. I did not. We were in the middle of nowhere with stops during the night. I must have managed a few hours' sleep, but I was not unhappy when morning came and I could determine where we were. Since Mark looked vey much like someone from the North, no one ever wanted to see his passport. Arrived back in built up villages or small towns, Mark was equally comfortable.

Malawi was special. It was cold. Yes, it gets very cold in some parts of Africa. I nearly froze in Swaziland. I also encountered a temperature in Zimbabwe of 3 degrees Celsius, and I was in Harare, the middle veldt. However, as everywhere I ventured in Africa, people were kind and helpful. I was reminded of the way we treated strangers (I do not mean tourists) who came by and asked for a glass of water. Here, my mode of transport was a helicopter. The President wanted our Human Rights mission to go well, and since we had little time, he used his helicopter to bring persons whose human rights were said to have been violated, to us. He also provided for us to visit lake Malawi, the deepest lake in the world and in several ways its most pristine.

I later learnt that there are some 600 species in the lake.

Finally come the three countries of the Sahel/Sahara Desert, Burkina Faso, Mali and Morocco. I stopped off for a few days in Burkina Faso on my return from Timbuktu to Bouaké. I stayed with a friend in Ouagadougou. The capital city was fairly typical of this dusty country. The wind constantly disturbs the laterite of its roads and blows off the little soil left in what is largely Sahel.

Yet, the biggest and sweetest tomatoes I have ever tasted came from here and in Mali. What was interesting was that in this country with the Blue, Red and Black Volta rivers, there was no immediate source of water between its northern frontier with Mali and Ouagadougou. So, water for planting was drawn from a well some 50 to 100 metres deep!

Mali, the neighbouring and much larger country, contains Timbuktu, which was once located on the Niger, where it turns North. It is difficult to envisage how important this city was before its capture by a Moroccan horde in 1591. Books were the chief item of sale sometime before, even though the gold trade from the South and the salt trade from the North passed through here. It still has a vast number of private libraries, whose books may have numbered as many as 250,000 manuscripts, some dating back to the 8th century.

Scholarship was so advanced that once, a Northern scholar who came to teach at the Sankoré University, had to return to the classroom to catch up with his students. Timbuktu at one time had some twenty-six textile factories along with its 25,000 students. Mali itself is not nearly as large as the ancient Mali Empire. The country stretches northward into the deep Sahara and is some 1.24 million square kilometres as compared with Western Europe's approximate 195,000 square kilometres.

Morocco is Mali's north-western neighbour. Unlike contemporary Mali, its western border is the Atlantic Ocean. It was named after its oldest known city,

Marrakesh, founded circa 1067. That city in its Almoravid glory was the centre of an Empire that covered all of contemporary Morocco, parts of Western Algeria and Southern Spain. When I visited Marrakesh, the old city (founded by early Muslims and its trade controlled by Jews who lived in a quarter just outside the city) was still partly there. Its Kasbah was even more impressive than that of Casa Blanca. It had remained the centre of a leather trade, which earned the name of the Moroccan leather used for binding books and the like. Marrakesh had a turbulent history as a result of its importance, constantly switching hands from one conqueror to the other.

Morocco seems also to have been peopled by humanoids about 3 million years ago, from which the Neanderthal of Europe may have emerged. This was in some ways odd, since most known early human development occurred in the Rift valley of Eastern Africa, which stretches from Ethiopia back down to South Africa.

The final area of travel, though not within Africa, has a very distinct African origin. As mentioned before, Anita and I spent our honeymoon in Cancun, where even hotels displayed the step pyramid building style of the Maya. There we visited Chichen Itza, normally translated as the mouth to the open well of Itza (presumably the name of a ruler), but translated by our driver to mean the open mouth of Itza, which would give it a definite Egyptian connection. In ancient Egypt, the dead man had his mouth opened to allow his spirit's egress. Chichen Itza was the last resort of the Mayan Empire before it fell apart.

The African connection of the Maya is significant. They were culturally descended from the Olmec, the Xi of West Africa. The Xi people were evidently Mande and had had connections with ancient Egypt. It took a long time before it could be accepted that they had come from sub-Saharan Africa. Linguists tried to tie their language to the Berbers and other North Africans. It was only when their anti-African bias disappeared and they tested the language against Mande that they were able to decipher the Mayan hieroglyphs. I asked our driver what the Mayan word for 'writing' was and he indicated that it was what sounded like the Mande word.

The Maya seem to have improved on the writing of the Olmec and wrote many books that the ignorant Spaniards burnt, including their book of origins, the Popul Vuh, which our driver felt had been tainted with Christianity. They also had the concept of zero as part of the simplest yet elaborate counting system in existence. They had symbols for one, five and zero, yet they could write down sums in the millions.

They not only built great step pyramids, palaces, temples and ball courts; they were also great astronomers, being able to predict eclipses with unerring accuracy: their combined calendars lost only one day in 4000 years! They seem to have been the first ones known to have grown maize, which spread throughout the Americas. They also had a very highly advanced medical system, which in 900 CE had secured a life expectancy of 54 years as compared to 29 years in contemporary France. They did brain surgery and had an advanced dental system. They were several million strong in 900 CE with some 1 million in Belize, just across the border from Mexico in the Yucatan Peninsula. Interestingly too, they were not the conventional empire although one talks of the Mayan Empire, but a collection of city states that covered Mexico, Belize, Honduras and Guatemala where Mirador (the largest of the step pyramids) lies high in the mountain forests of that country.

Africa was of great importance to me, as indeed it should be to everyone. It is where humanity evolved; it is where civilisation first blossomed; it is where the religions that we now practise were born. It is also not a place simply of poverty and war. It is now becoming the hub of some new technologies and there will be many African countries in the next decade or two which will be more attractive than our island homes.

Since then, I continued to teach Governance part-time at the University until recently. After my departure from UWI, I was appointed Chairman of the Barbados Agricultural and Marketing Corporation and that takes enough of my time in what I consider a very important effort to make us more food sufficient as well as innovative.

The bridge playing has developed into what seems to

be a permanent affair, moving one afternoon a week from one of our homes to another. We are two teams of four consisting apart from myself of Vernon Smith, Sir Errol (Mickey) Walrond, Edward Walcott, my cousin Roger Marville, his sister Shirley and one make up person. For some reason I cannot quite fathom, my team of Roger and Edward and my partner and I almost invariably win. The games also provide ample opportunity for discussing whatever is of topical importance. The teams at one time included Sir Frederick and of Dr. Jordan, both of whom have passed on; but the game continues.

Looking back, I have had a great life so far. I have travelled to places many people have never even dreamed about. In the process, I have met several of the people I have admired and have had the opportunity to work with including Bajans like Professor Cardinal Warde; to serve in our Senate and to be the Representative of the country which I love, Barbados. What seems sad to me is that with a group of prominent friends, I grew up in what I now see as the golden age of Barbados; but we were never able to prolong that age.

Other Titles by R. Orlando Marville